The Woman behind the Paint:
Artwork, Words, Womanhood, and a Recovery

by

Colleen Kassner

With an Introduction by Rachel Forman, Grand Avenue Club

"My art is more than painting a picture. For me, it is a way to honor my recovery and record my progress as a human-being and an artist."

Colleen Kassner

The Woman behind the Art

at

Grand Avenue Club

Grand Avenue Club (GAC) in Milwaukee boasts a thriving Employment Program, whereby scores of people are working out in the community; a fine Supported Education Program, whereby members are earning vocational certificates and degrees at local schools; and an Evening, Weekend, and Holiday Programming whereby members celebrate every holiday, see movies and plays; organize baseball games and dances; attend concerts, sports events, and festivals out in the community; go to local museums and spend some very cozy times with each other at GAC.

GAC also has its own art gallery, a spacious, beautifully illuminated room on the fourth floor of our 24,000 square foot building. Gallery Grand was founded shortly after Colleen joined us as a volunteer in 2006. It is fueled by her energy, intensity, talent, and her splendid capacity for relationships both with the GAC community as well as her large and eclectic network of friends who are gallery owners, artists, photographers, musicians, and poets.

I first met Colleen many years ago when she came to GAC as a University of Wisconsin-Milwaukee undergraduate working toward a degree in social work. In 1995/96 Colleen was assigned to work alongside members and staff in Grand Avenue Club's Clerical Unit. Colleen was one of scores of social work students who have done internships here at GAC over the past 24 years. She did a good job, expressed great enthusiasm for the GAC approach, and did well at her internship.

After she completed her time with us, we didn't see or hear from Colleen for nearly ten years. Remembering her enthusiasm for all things GAC, I used to pass the art deco apartment building where she had lived in with her daughter and think to myself, "What ever happened to Colleen? She was so enthusiastic about GAC."

Aware for some time that several members and at least one staff member at GAC did art, I wanted to develop something to promote their interests. In June 2006, just before Colleen joined us, we exhibited the work of GAC artists in the rotunda of the U.S. Federal Court House on Wisconsin Avenue in Milwaukee.

Shortly after this Colleen called GAC and asked two questions: "Do you remember me?"—and—"Would GAC be interested in doing something with art?" "It was a resounding "Yes!" to both.

Colleen re-joined our community as a volunteer and we organized "the GAC Art Collective," which consisted of both members and staff from GAC as well as artists and photographers from the community. In those early days she and I talked frequently about how art done by people with mental illness was often viewed as different from the art done by others. I had on my bookshelves and had read or skimmed epic tomes with titles like *The Art of the Mentally Ill*. I had also attended art shows organized by mental health advocacy organizations that called attention to the diagnosis, hospitalizations, and severity of the illness of the people whose work was displayed.

In our conversations about art, Colleen and I both rejected the insistence on a focus on pathology in the art produced by members of our community. We also rejected the idea that art activities at GAC would be seen as "art therapy"—an explicit effort to use art to get to some underlying condition or need for personal change in the lives of GAC colleagues. Here is what Colleen and I became so excited about together: GAC Art Collective and Gallery Grand would integrate the art of the members and staff of GAC with the art of other local artists. We decided to disregard the prevailing doctrine of "art done by sick people." Our message would be "look at the art."

Gallery Grand is now nine years old and has had a huge impact on the quality of life in our community. Colleen has mentored and exhibited the work of many GAC artists, encouraged them to expand their audiences, and has always reserved exhibit space for GAC artists who work independently in a home studio. She has been the driving force behind GAC's consistent and successful participation in Milwaukee's Gallery Night and Day, drawing Gallery Grand into the network of galleries that are open to the public several weekends a year. She is an effective and enthusiastic salesperson of art from our gallery in a city that cannot boast of a strong "art buying" tradition as part of the civic landscape. In addition, the walls of GAC's home, a stately and architecturally significant building in the center of Milwaukee, are filled with original art by GAC members, staff, and Colleen. The group and individual portraits that she has painted of our members, which are part of our "permanent collection," have done so much for the self-esteem of our members and the aesthetics of our home.

Colleen is a woman of great talent. I'm thrilled that she has thrived so beautifully within the GAC community. I'm fascinated with her most recent project, a series of paintings of her very own sisterhood of talented artists who are also soulful women. I look forward to whatever work she may do in the future. As far as I'm concerned, she is a star of Milwaukee's artistic community, for she is not only an artist of increasing talent, but also a person who has created a rich and rewarding cultural life for the GAC community, including me.

Rachel Forman, Grand Avenue Club

It Started with a "Smooch"

Colleen Kassner

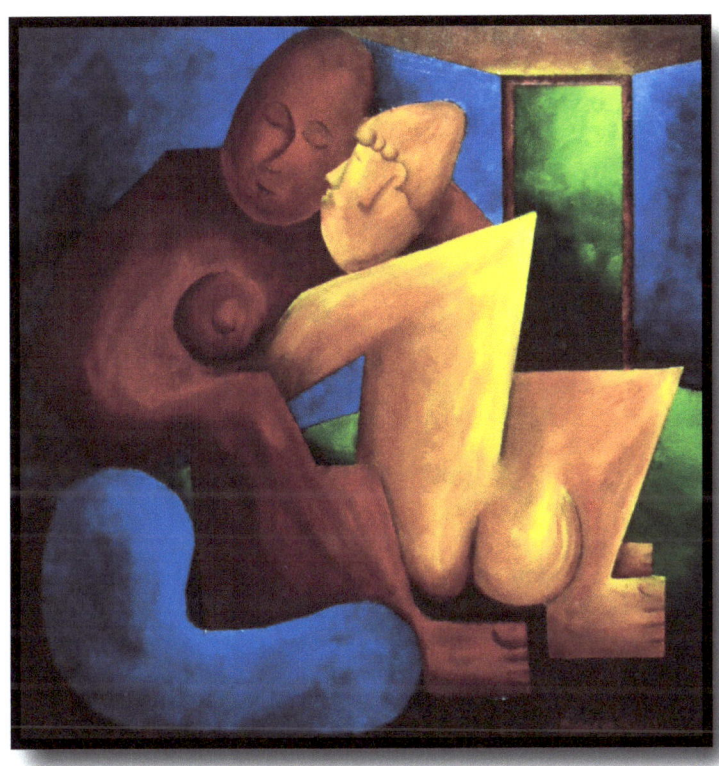

Smooch, ca. 2001
(In the artist's collection)

When does creativity begin?

When other little girls were playing with dolls, I was using crayons. The colors excited my imagination. Visualizing how beautifully I would draw the dolls and the pretty clothes they would wear, I fantasized someday becoming a famous designer. The teachers in grade school always called me a dreamer. But, isn't that the essence of being an artist?

I grew up and continued to dream. After dealing with depression, a divorce, alcohol abuse, and later being diagnosed with bipolar disorder, that little girl drawing the dolls needed to come out.

It took an extremely traumatic psychiatric hospitalization to release the creativity again. After the hospitalization, Philo, (then my boyfriend, now my husband,) encouraged me to go into the spare room to paint. He felt it would make me feel better. A recently found picture from that time shows me sitting at the desk looking happy, with watercolors in hand and some of my very earliest works surrounding me. Little did I know art was to become my life and that the dreams of a little girl would come true.

Philo and I met at "Poet's Monday" in 1994. We were both writers at the time. He was cute: a poet, an artist, a photographer. My kind of a guy! He was to become my source of strength in recovery. We were friends at first, enjoying easy conversations about life, poetry, art, our daughters, and our youth. We developed a comfortable relationship that evolved into a romance. We felt that we were made for each other. My family adored him; my daughter, Briana, thought he was "cool." We laughed...a lot.

While studying at the University of Wisconsin—Milwaukee to earn a degree in social welfare, my social-work internship was with Grand Avenue Club (GAC.) It was a good match because GAC is a work and education-oriented community of adults who have experienced mental illness and my skills fit its program. The executive director, Rachel Forman, was a strong role model and she pushed me to achieve. I made Dean's List that year with a 3.8 grade point average. However, the stress and pressures started to take a toll on my stability. After not drinking for several years, alcohol re-entered the picture. Drinking was starting to interfere with my education and causing problems with my daughter and with Philo. He gave me an ultimatum: either quit drinking or leave. Alcohol won and we broke up.

The next 18 months were the most difficult and loneliest period of my life. Alcohol started to take over and life became unmanageable. With the exception of school and my daughter, the rest of my wonderful world gradually disappeared. I lost contact with Grand Avenue Club, the poetry scene, and Philo. My social sphere circled around bars, parties, late nights, and endless days of hangovers. My anticipated spring 1998 graduation was postponed until December, 1998 because multiple psychiatric hospitalizations prevented me from finishing the course work.

The following fall semester I graduated with a respectable grade point average. However, the years of hard work and effort seemed meaningless. I was still unstable and self-medicating with alcohol. The future looked hopeless. In the spring of 1999, I received a letter from Philo. That letter prompted the resumption of our relationship.

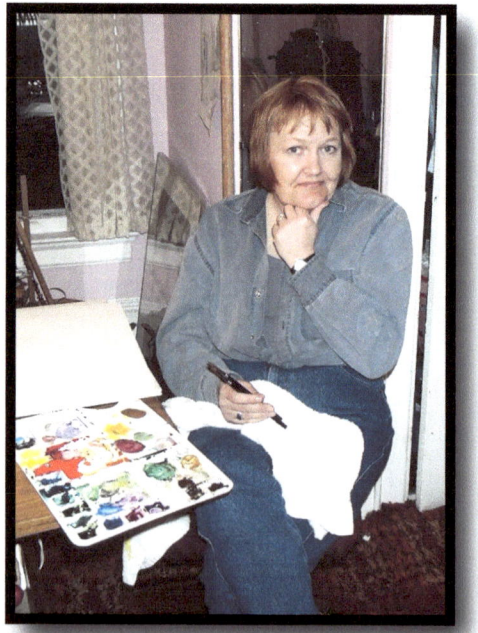

In my first studio, 2001.

A Little Romance

Philo and I rekindled our romance. My daughter graduated from high school and was ready to be on her own. I moved in with Philo during the spring of 2000 after agreeing to quit drinking, which turned out to be difficult but not impossible. This time, I was really ready. A life with Philo was more important than booze. I was somewhat successful. After going for weeks without drinking, the urge for a martini would take over. I would "sneak drink," naively thinking that Philo wouldn't know. Even though this meant jeopardizing my still precarious relationship with him, I thought I could pull it off.

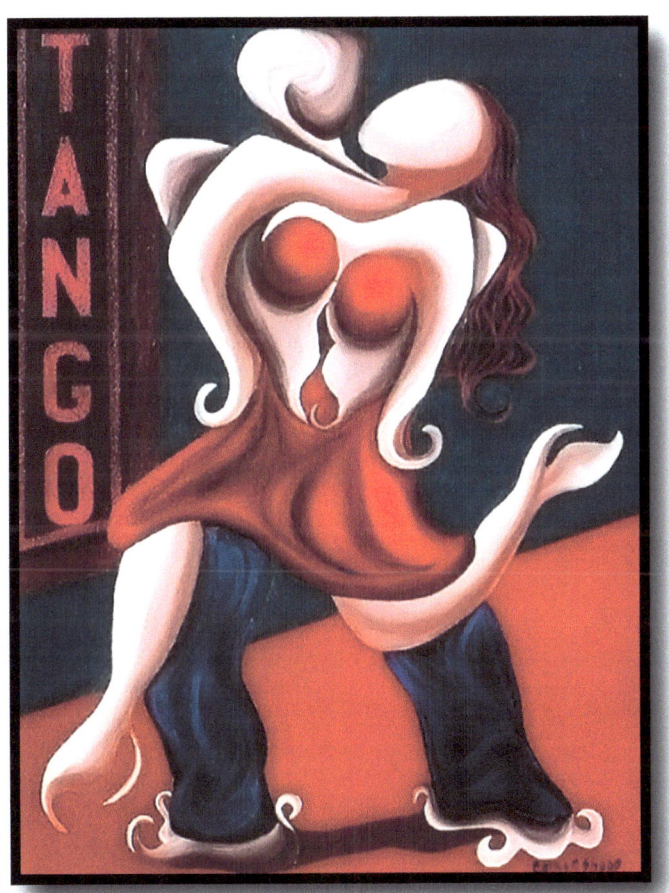

Medication is an integral part of treating mental illness and mine was a mess. Between 1999 and 2001 my psychiatrist had me on an average of fourteen separate medications simultaneously. There was a shoe box filled with medications on my bedside table. There were pills for sleep, others for pain, some slowed me down and some picked me up. One was even for Alzheimer's. I forgot what they were but they were all prescribed by the same doctor. Going in and out of the psychiatric hospital every few months and in a day treatment program the rest of the time, I had become a "professional patient." Philo and I thought that this was going to be the story of our lives.

When I was in for yet another hospitalization, Philo took matters into his own hands. He looked at the boxes of medication bottles and realized that something was seriously wrong. He went to the doctor's office with me and demanded to know the purpose of each medication and why it was prescribed. The doctor didn't know. With Philo's encouragement I found a new doctor. In 2001, I was put in the hospital for two weeks to titrate off all the medications and be placed on a new regimen of only two medications. Finally, I was heading in the right direction.

Tango ca. 2002
(In a private collection)

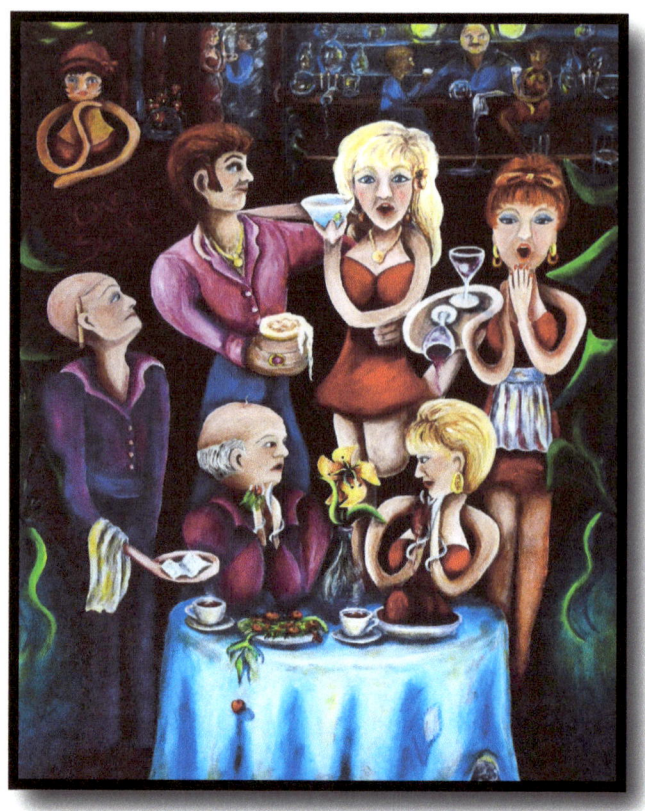

Chéz Swirl, ca. 2012

At this same time and more importantly, a major shift in my self-awareness was taking place. I was coming alive; the spark of my creative drive was reignited after the fog of years of over-medication had lifted. I was re-connecting with art, with the little girl drawing dolls. Art therapy in the hospital was an effective means of expression for me so I began to do the therapy on my own. Spending my hospital evenings in my room with a sketch pad I would draw for hours on end, filling pages of the pads of paper until I was tired enough to go to sleep. The walls of my room were covered with my drawings, some of which I still have. Art was giving me the clarity that would become the defining focus of my life.

A few days after leaving the hospital, feeling human again and slightly invincible, I thought I'd like to have a drink. So, while I was out and about, I stopped in a bistro and ordered a martini. I sipped. When I realized stupid I was being, how much I risked losing, and just how tired I was of jeopardizing my fragile and precious stability. I set the drink down, left a generous tip, and never touched a drop again. The compulsion no longer owned me nor had power over me. I was finally free...free to recover.

After this epiphany, I began to paint in earnest. After dabbling at first with a watercolor here and a canvas there, the mood stabilizing effects of doing art began to take hold and I began to take creating art seriously. Art focused my thoughts outward and gave me a means of expressing myself and channeling my "manic energies" on self-affirming pursuits rather than self-annihilation. My days were spent learning the myriad of techniques necessary to work with acrylics. I learned about the different qualities of pigments, how mediums worked, how to stretch a canvas, and how to layer the colors and mix them for different effects. Canvas after canvas was painted...the majority of them awful...except for *Smooch*. I painted it on a day while Philo was at work. He came home, saw the painting, and from that point forward knew that art was going to be the focus of my life. Art—that little girl drawing dolls—was giving me my confidence back, offering me a sense of control and destiny.

In 2002 I had a showing of my early work at a Milwaukee gallery called Cora Dora. In it were *Smooch*, and the *Dinner and Dancing* series, of which *Tango* is a part. I remember the opening and how my knees shook as I watched the people pouring into the gallery to look at the art. It was art I had created and people were appreciating it!

In 2004, after a couple of years of stability and development of my skills, I was offered a solo showing at a coffee shop called "Ruby G's." The paintings *Pea Slurp* and *Geez Ruby* were done during this time. Both pieces were a take-off on Philo and me and the lighthearted side of our romance. Having a receptive venue for my art was a great experience. I kept busy doing new shows and producing new work every three months. My friends also showed work and together we all learned a lot about presentation, installation, and marketing.

In spite of all this, something was lacking. A piece of the puzzle was still missing. I loved my social worker roots and I missed helping people improve their lives. My artwork needed an expanded audience so I decided to do an art/exhibit benefit for a non-profit organization. It would reconnect me to those roots and give me a larger audience at the same time. Grand Avenue Club was the first place that came to mind. Ten years after leaving my internship and living through so many traumas, I contacted Rachel Forman to ask if she would like to do an art benefit for Grand Avenue Club. She was delighted and quite surprised to hear from me. She enthusiastically said, "Yes!"

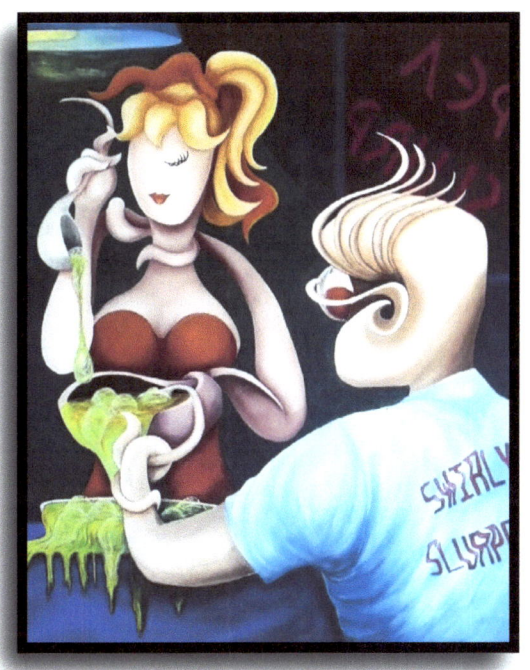

Pea Slurp, 2005

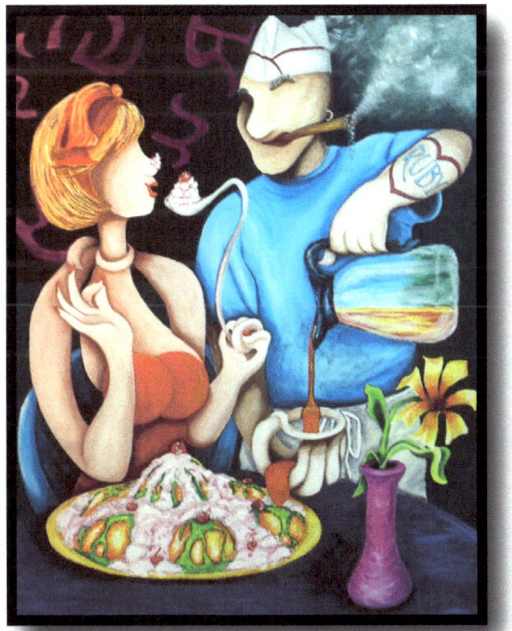

We did a three-day benefit at Ruby G's in September of 2006. On Friday night, we had the art opening and reception for the GAC artists. On Saturday evening, we featured music; and on Sunday afternoon, we organized a show of spoken word and performance art. It was a success. This event would define my future.

Geez Ruby, 2005
(In a private collection)

The Chelsea Hotel

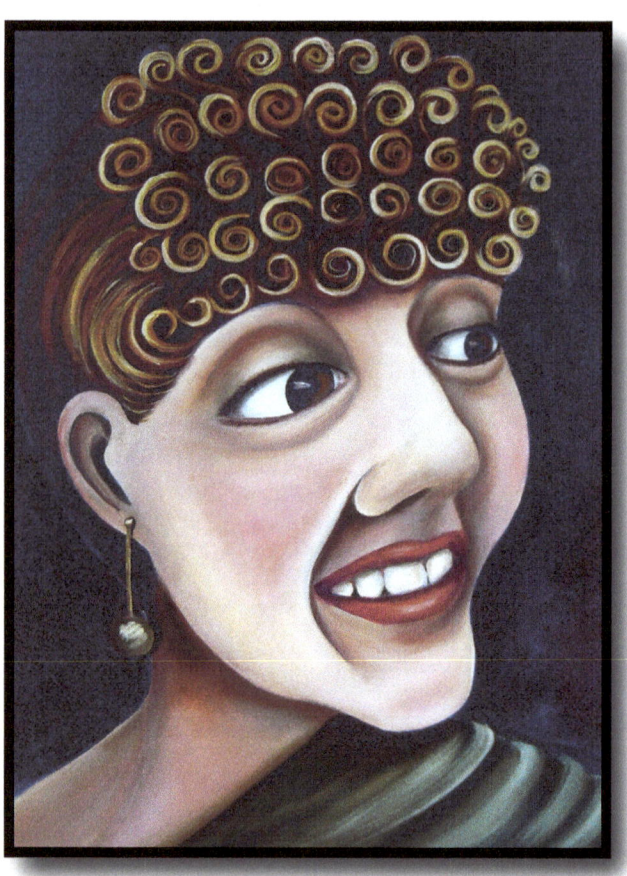

Chelsea Belle ca. 2008/9
(In a private collection)

Philo took me to stay at the iconic Chelsea Hotel in Manhattan on a dare. I had only been to New York for brief periods in 1969 and 1972. This was 2004 and things had changed drastically since those years...except for the Chelsea Hotel. The hotel had a rich history of artists and bohemians who graced its halls and rooms. We stayed there for four consecutive vacations until the hotel was sold. After the sale, the colorful artists and people were either evicted or moved out. Now, it is being converted to a "boutique" hotel. I don't think Janis Joplin would approve.

When we arrived at the Chelsea, I was agog at the funkiness of the hotel. To say it was colorful is an understatement. We checked in and settled into our shabby, chrome-yellow painted room, with nails in the walls for our clothing, tattered drapes, a lumpy and quite squeaky mattress, and threadbare carpet. We awoke early the next morning and ventured down to the lobby. The late night revelers were returning home.

Upon entering the lobby, we were greeted by a drag queen sauntering in from his night's performance, sans wig and in full make-up, a peacock colored, sequined mini dress, and six inch stilettos—replete with fish-net stockings.

Who needs Broadway when you have the lobby of the Chelsea Hotel?

Artists also loved and lived in the Chelsea. In the center of the hotel was a 10 story iron-balustrade staircase that was lined top to bottom with paintings collected in lieu of back-rent. We would take the elevator up to the 10th floor then walk the staircase down to the lobby. The halls echoed with our footsteps as the ghosts and history of past tenants followed us down the stairs.

The lobby was the main-stage of the Chelsea. The artists, residents, and many guests would congregate there to people watch, chat, and see–and–be–seen. One artist in particular, the "Artiste" as we called him, would set up his easel in the lobby, sketch books at his side, and squint carefully at his canvas as he "worked." It was quite a show. However, I later observed that the whole time he was at his canvas there was never any paint on his brush—it's the audience that counts at the Chelsea. Another artist would wait until he saw a guest in the lobby and then pull out his cell phone and proceed to call his "agent" about his latest art deal. He would be mid-conversation about the megabucks he was making on the deal, and if the hotel guest would get up to leave, he would snap the phone shut until the next person would arrive and the performance would start again.

Some of the stories at the Chelsea are funny and some poignantly sad. There was a woman; we called her the "Teacher," who would sit in the lobby for hours reading to an imaginary class of children from the imaginary book in her hand. She was quite animated while reading and I'm sure to her, the children were very real.

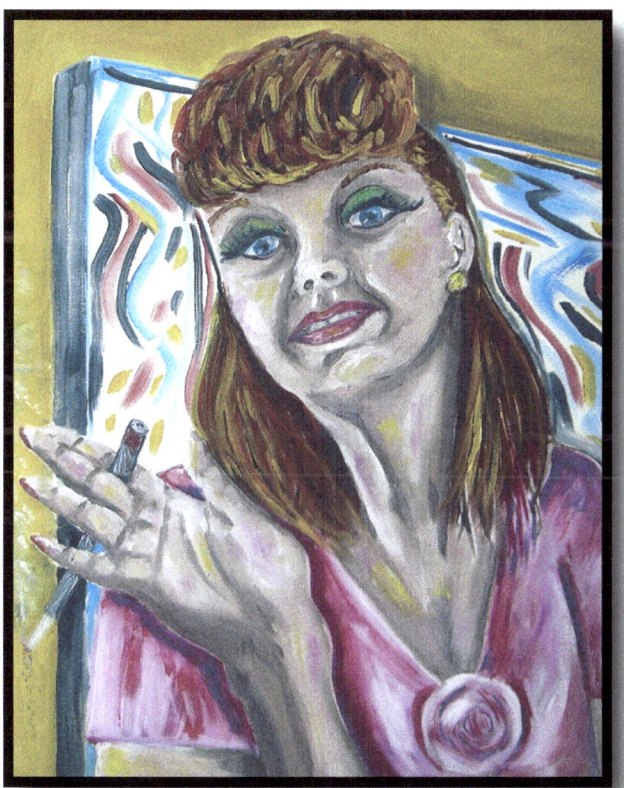

A year later, when we returned to the Chelsea, Philo and I had a room next to hers. Ours, though shabby, was clean with a bed and sheets. In hers was a soiled and bare mattress on a cot. The nicotine stains and odor permeated the decor of broken blinds, peeling paint, and dirt encrusted windows. The following year when we stayed at the Chelsea, she was gone.

Philo and I genuinely loved the Chelsea Hotel and dearly miss the chaotic entertainment of its lobby and its plethora of interesting and quirky tenants. Our stays there stimulated this series of paintings. Although there are only a few they are based either on real people or composites of people we would see while relaxing in the ever-changing lobby. *Chelsea Belle* is a whimsical interpretation of the women we would see in the hotel. *Cha-Cha La-Roux* is totally fictional; however, I have decided that she was a down-and-out "Rockette" living out the rest of her years in a one room apartment in the Chelsea Hotel—something that is a real possibility.

Cha-Cha LaRoux
ca. 2009

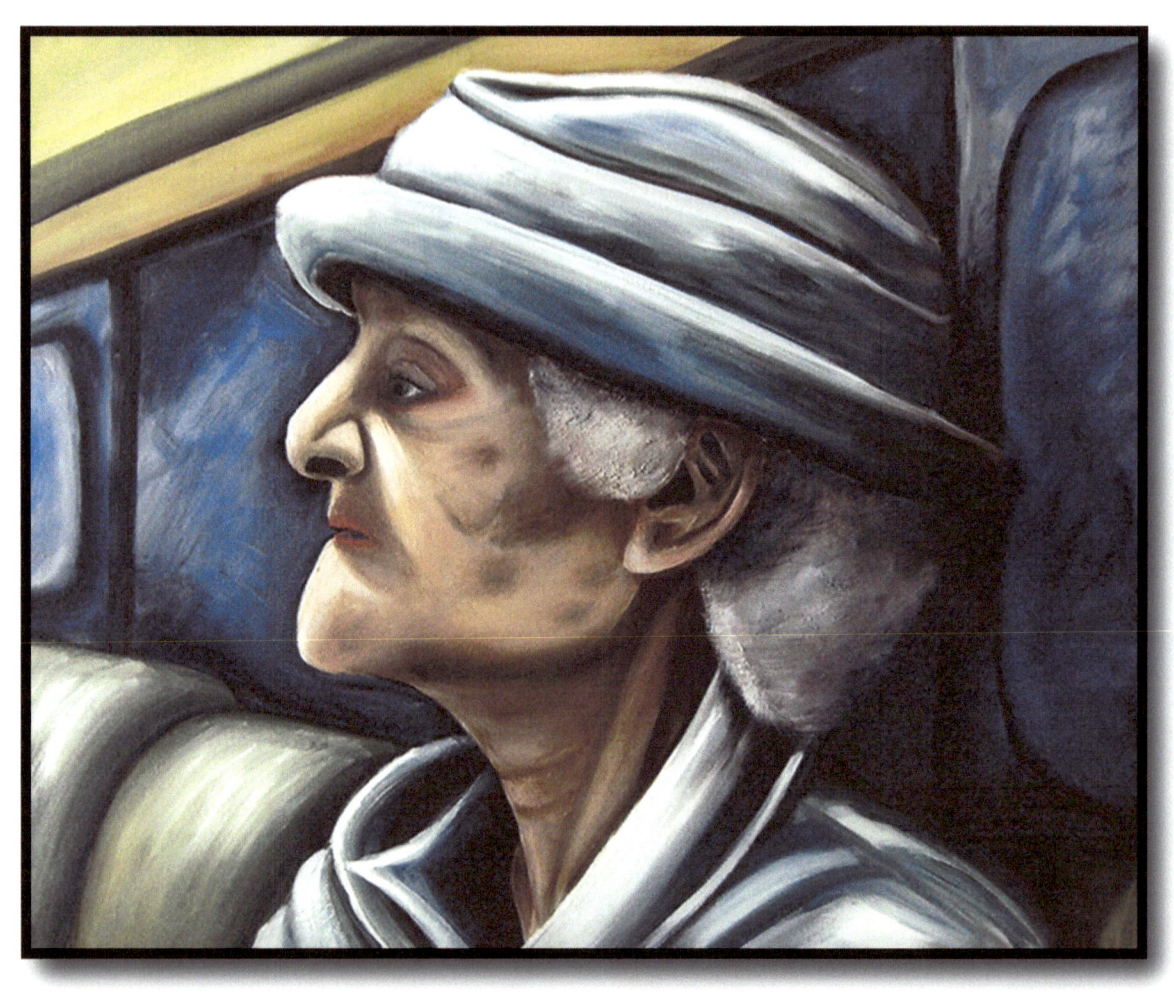

Stormé DeLarverie, ca. 2009
(In a private collection)

Stormé DeLarverie

At one of our stays, while whiling away afternoon hours in the world's best lobby, we saw her. We called her the "Pshew" lady. As we were watching the assorted characters meander in and out, we saw an old woman who looked somewhat like the Art Carney character, "Crazy Guggenheim," leave the hotel. She had on well-worn army boots, a tattered denim shirt, and a denim hat that had seen better days. We didn't think much of it. We saw her all the time. A few hours later, the woman came through the front door of the hotel in the weaving dance step of inebriation. We could see her eyes aiming for the elevator located at the far end of the lobby. Her focus was intense as she navigated the obstacle course of hotel furniture, area rugs, suitcases and planters that seemed to jump in front of her as she zigzagged through the lobby. Her dance was well timed and when she arrived at the reception desk she let out an audible, "Pshew!"

One of the residents yelled out, "Hello, Stormé."

That was our introduction to one of the most interesting people we met at the Chelsea. Stormé DeLarverie was a well-loved, long term resident of the hotel. She had lived there for nearly 40 years when we met her. Her colorful past was not obvious, but, one evening she shared her amazing history with us. Stormé had been the drag-king emcee in the drag-queen extravaganza, "The Jewel Box Review." In the 1950's and 60's she traveled throughout the United States and Europe with the "Review." She was of mixed race and, often in the US, had to "pass" in order to get into the venues. At 89 years old, she still "packed heat." She was once the body-guard for the photographer Diane Arbus's children. She is purported to be the person who threw the first punch at the 1969 Stonewall Inn Riots in Greenwich Village. Her presence there is credited, either through lore or fact, with launching the "gay rights" movement. She was a pioneer in the movement and well respected by the LGBT community.

She died in a nursing home in Brooklyn on May 24, 2014 at the age of 94. I am happy to have had the privilege of knowing her and creating a portrait of her that confers respect and dignity to such an interesting person.

The "Manic" Series:
Power in an Image

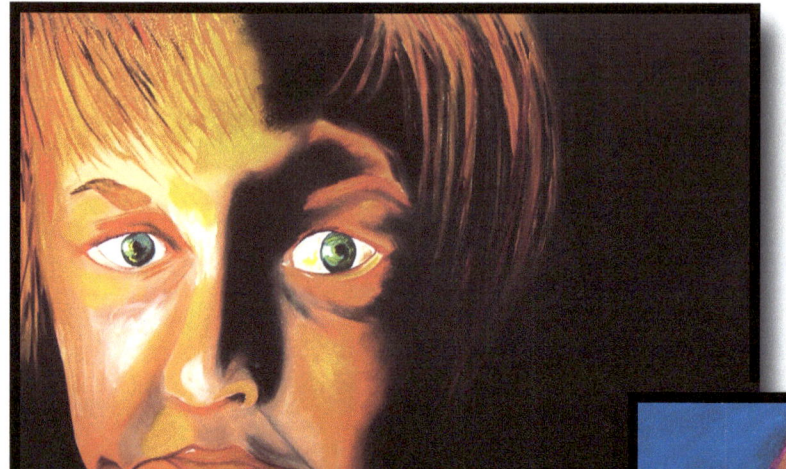

In 2007, after the success of the benefit, I began to volunteer at GAC. At first it was to help out with a few creative projects. Eventually, talk ensued of a gallery for Grand Avenue Club. We decided to do a large show, to be presented in June of 2007, featuring the work of a New York artist. We hung, promoted

Thoughtful
(In a private collection)

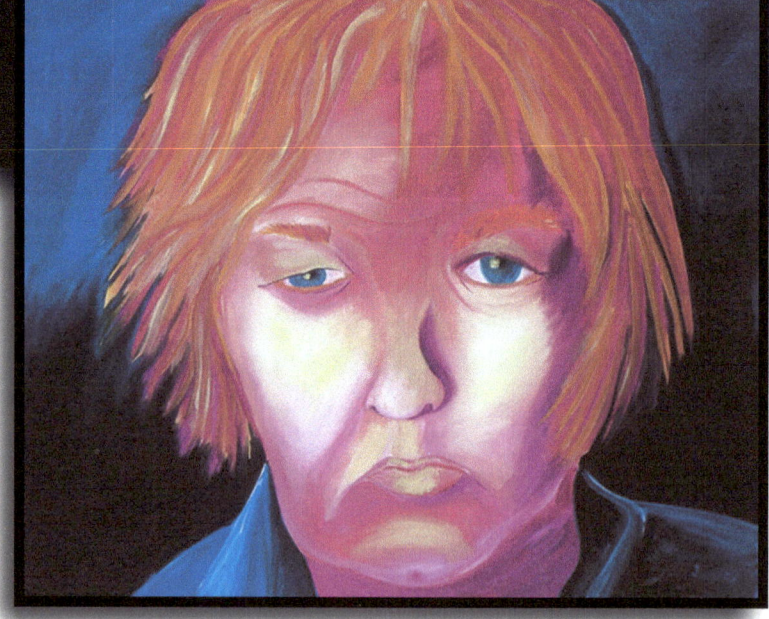

and sold a large portion of what she brought. It helped to launch the "idea" of art at GAC. Philo also began to volunteer at this time, helping with the art show and fixing GAC's many computers. Philo and I worked to put together an international, digital presentation of artwork from Clubhouses world-wide to be shown at the 14th International Clubhouse Seminar that was held in Milwaukee during

Angry

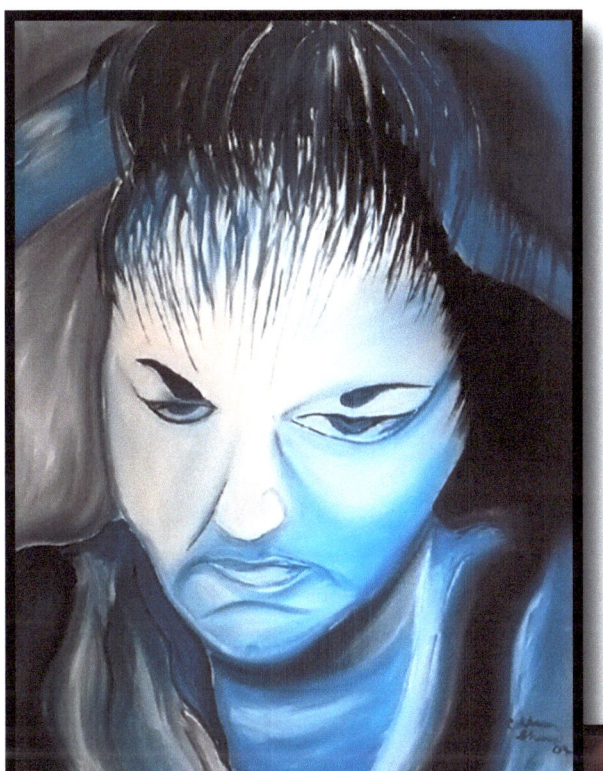

Blue Woman

the following October. Philo compiled a catalog and I coordinated a simultaneous show in what was to become the Gallery Grand @ GAC. Art was becoming a popular part of GAC's many activities.

During this time I rediscovered a series of photos taken by Philo of me during my final manic episode. (Most boyfriends would call a doctor...mine grabbed his camera.) The photos covered only a fifteen minute time span but expressed a myriad of emotions. The photos themselves weren't very usable. However, I sensed they would make interesting paintings. They became a turning point for me, both in my art and in my mental health.

Creating these paintings, some of my earliest oils, was an intense experience. The process was visceral, causing me to relive the emotions of my mania as I worked the compositions. The paint flew onto the canvas; the images emerged as if they had a life of their own. The pain, the confusion, the exhaustion of the episode left my psyche and became the painting

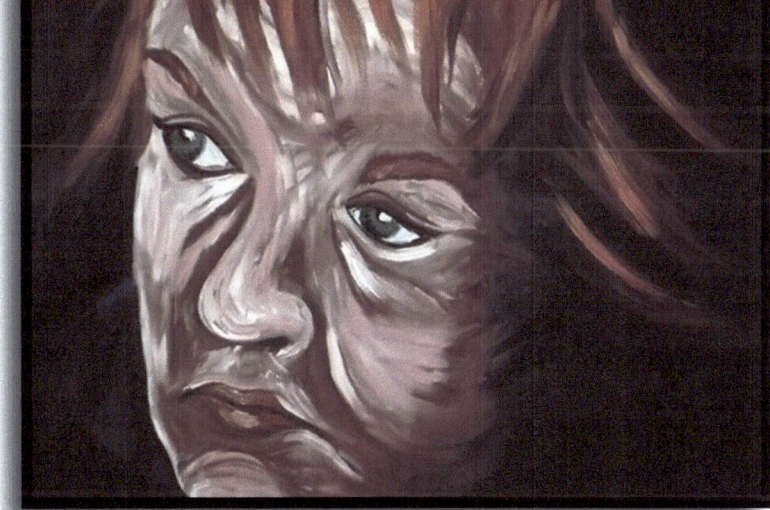

Done

Empty

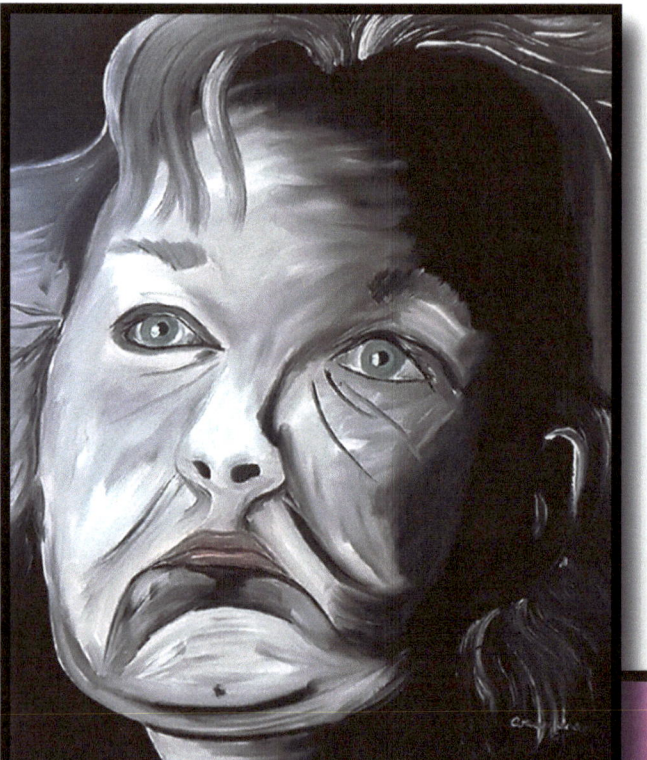

in front of me. I was experiencing mania again, but without the sadness, guilt, and horror of the aftermath. I was painting with a sense of clarity I had never felt before. These paintings were a symbolic farewell to my previous life of strife and chaos. They were also a beginning because they celebrated my emergence as a woman who was now capable of harnessing her own energies and creativity. They allowed me to say a final good-bye to the years that were and a warm hello to what was to become.

The *Manic* series taught me about the power of an image. We presented the works at a show in April of 2008. Many people came up to me at the opening to tell me stories of theirs, or a friend's, or a loved one's struggle with mental illness. The portraits helped them see their personal experiences through my work. It was affirming to see something that I created, that I expressed through art, have this impact on others. The power that is within an image, the ability of a painting to reach into a person's being, is what inspired me to move forward with portraiture.

Yellow Woman

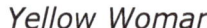

I proposed an idea to Rachel Forman. I would paint pictures of members. These would not be pictures of the "mentally ill" as they have sometimes been portrayed by other artists. These portraits would show the members, my friends and colleagues, as I had come to know them; people with lives, with desires to belong, to be productive, and to have meaning in the world. The paintings would tell the story of their experiences with mental illness, both their triumphs and their struggles.

In early 2010 we wrote a grant to the Mary Nohl Fund of the Greater Milwaukee Foundation to support *The Portrait Project: Faces of Resilience."*

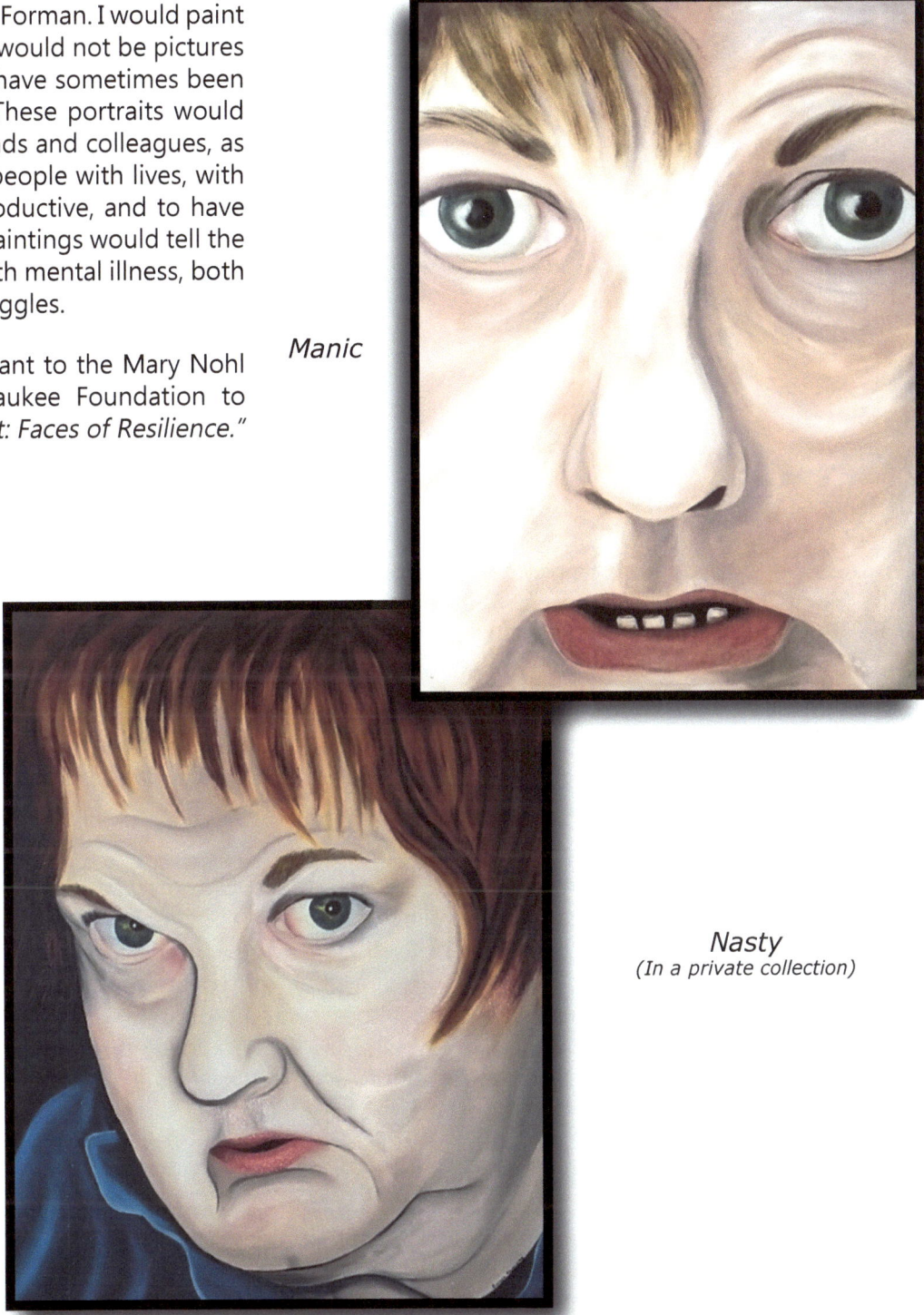

Manic

Nasty
(In a private collection)

The Portrait Projects

at

Grand Avenue Club

On Sunday, May 23, 2010, after having known each other for 15 years, Philo and I were married in the Gallery Grand @ GAC. We were surrounded by people who loved us and had seen us through so much. Our poet friend, Tim Kloss, performed the ceremony. Philo's family, my family, our family of friends from GAC and our wonderful artist-friends celebrated the occasion with great joy. Having the wedding in the gallery and being surrounded by so many people important to us, in a place so meaningful to us, gave the day a special significance.

In mid-June GAC was awarded, through the Greater Milwaukee Foundation, a Mary Nohl grant to fund *The Portrait Project: Faces of Resilience*. Mary Nohl was a Milwaukee, Wisconsin artist who, upon her death, left a generous endowment with the Greater Milwaukee Foundation, a portion of which funds artists working with non-profits. I felt honored to be able to work under this grant.

GAC was able to commission me to paint 15-20 portraits of GAC members within the course of a year. At this point my portraiture experience had been limited to a few rudimentary paintings of friends from my earlier work and the more emotional canvasses of the *Manic* series. *The Portrait Project: Faces of Resilience* was an exhilarating although daunting new challenge for me. I wanted the portraits to give voice and credence to a group of people, my friends and colleagues, who deserved recognition. So often, when living with a mental illness, a person is ignored, shunned, or trivialized. I wanted these portraits to change that. At first, many members were shy about participating. As the project progressed the enthusiasm grew. Many of the people I chose to paint were members with whom I worked on a daily basis, some were selected because of their history with GAC, and some because I found them endearing. All of them were important; all of them had stories to tell. The biographies we collected from them to accompany the portraits were moving, empowering, and often heartbreaking. Underneath the stories, behind the paintings, were the lives of the members, people who lived with mental illness, who survived and thrived through their community—GAC. If I could catch an inkling of this in the painting, I would be happy.

This project was a monumental undertaking. I had no idea how complex and intricate creating a portrait can become. Many times, half-way through the portrait, I would hate how it looked, set it aside and start over; often several times. I was learning a lot. My perseverance with the project and my drive to complete it as best I could consumed most of my time for the entire year. My studio was filled with the canvasses of GAC members staring at me, all in various stages of completion, silently waiting to tell their story. While working on the paintings I developed an intimacy with the entire process of painting; the canvas, oils, and brushes contributed to the person I was portraying. I was developing a new fondness and respect for the members of GAC.

The Portrait Project: Faces of Resilience was difficult, rewarding, frustrating, and one of the greatest learning experiences of my life. I will be forever thankful for the opportunity to create the work that addresses such an important topic; the elimination of the stigma surrounding mental illness.

The portraits were presented at Milwaukee's Gallery Night and Day in July 2011. I then had the honor of having them grace the lobby of the Milwaukee Repertory Theater for the duration of their production of the Broadway musical, *"next to normal."* They are now housed in the reception area of GAC as part of their permanent art collection.

THE PORTRAIT PROJECT : FACES OF RESILIENCE

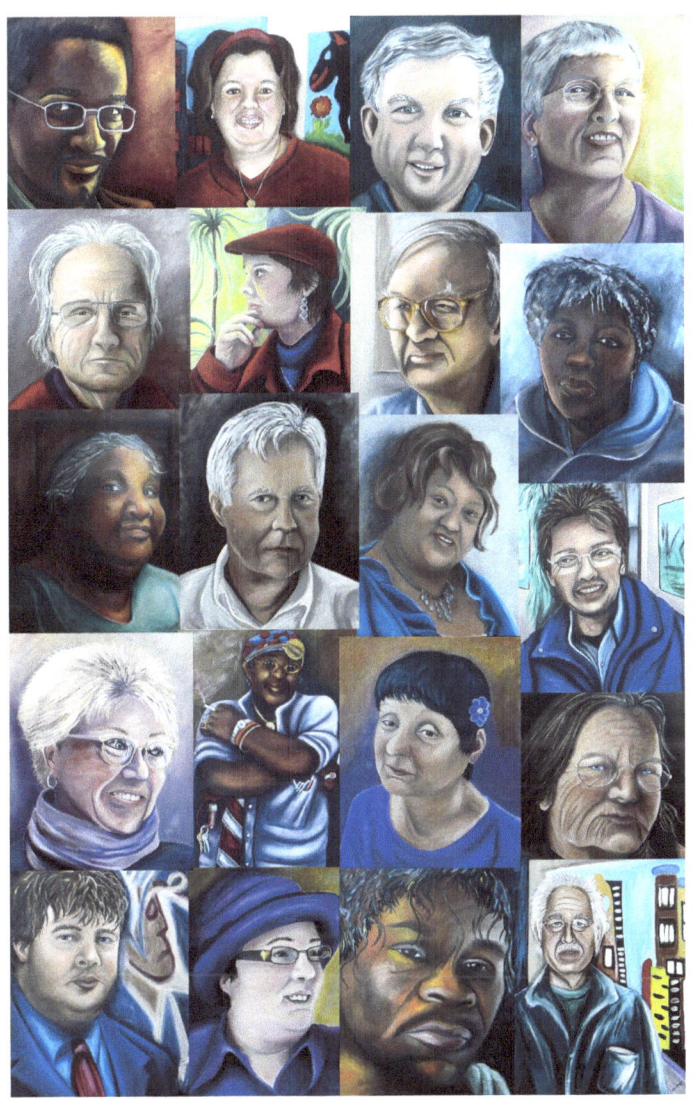

COLLEEN KASSNER 2010-2011
GALLERY GRAND @ GAC

Individual Portraits
(left to right: top to bottom)
Gerald Lloyd, Tracy Dreher, Brian Gumma, Deb Love
Dano Peterson, Ann Paszkiewicz Krachtt,
Louis Poore, Dorothy Cannady
Janet McCray, Greg John, Cheryl Banks, Kenny Gumb
Roxanne Rozek, Michael Bivens, Sherry Ybanez, Trixie Morse
Rory McKeown, Shoshana Elias, Jonathan Fields, Thomas Tadyshak

Painting the Life of GAC

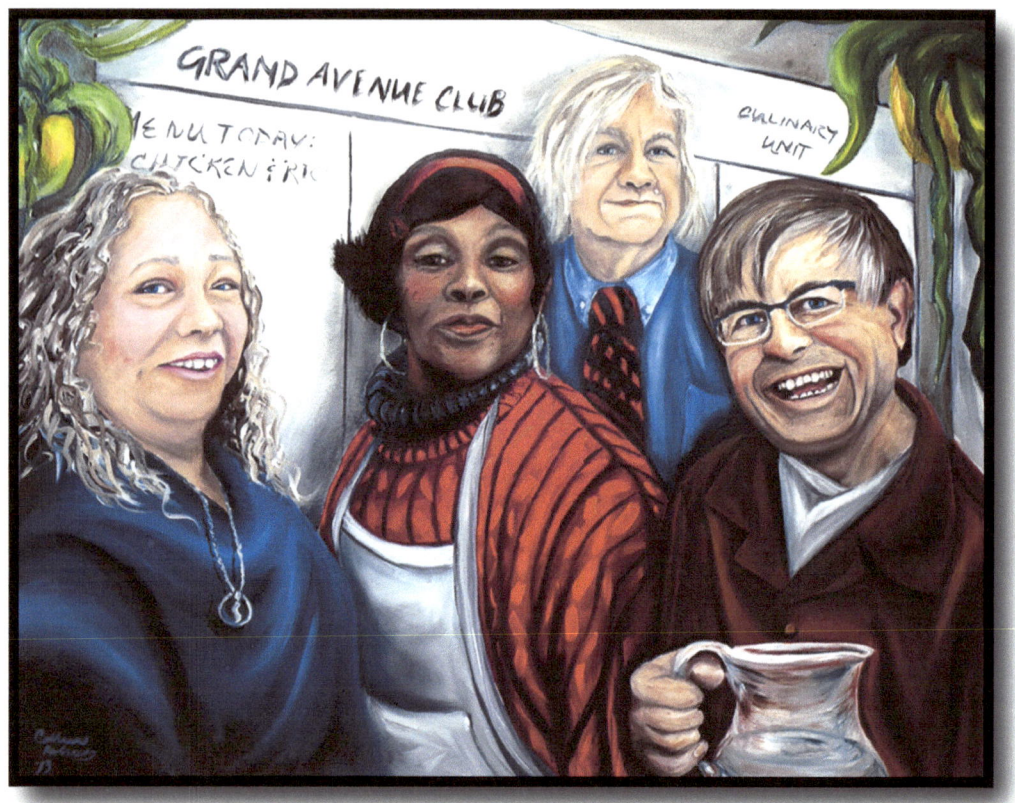

In the Cafeteria

Pictured from left to right: Martha Van Norman, Lashawanda Allen, Dale Hester, Steve Keil

The Portrait Project: Faces of Resilience told a powerful story of individual recovery. However, there was much more to convey. In 2012 GAC applied for and was granted another Mary Nohl Grant to create four group portraits of members working within GAC. By the end of the one year grant period, six were produced. Both phases of the project were to be combined in a book written by Rachel Forman and me entitled, *Facing Forward: An Artist, a Community, and Stories of Resilience.*

GAC's primary function is to give all its members, adults who have experienced mental illness, the opportunity to find their way back into the world of employment. GAC does this by offering meaningful work experiences, educational opportunities, and a support system that makes the transition from psychiatric patient to a fully participating member of society possible. In this phase of the project, I wanted to document the important work done by members at GAC by portraying them doing daily tasks in the work units that keep GAC thriving. The opportunity to participate in a meaningful way, with work that is vital to this energetic community, is the inspiration behind these paintings.

Many GAC members have important stories to tell. Some members come to GAC after many hospitalizations, years of illness, and lives in disarray, many having lost the support of family and loved ones in the process. Some are more fortunate and have family and other loved ones to assist and encourage them. They all arrive though, like my charcoal drawing on the canvas, with an outline of what is to become. The people I portrayed in these paintings are of different races, religions and ages. Some are young adults and others are coming into the later years of their lives. They are all vital human beings with the same needs for acceptance and success that is a part of the human condition. Helping them achieve their own definition of success is what the GAC community is about.

The group portraits were a tremendous challenge. I had many elements to consider. There were anywhere from four to seven different people and personalities to capture. There were environments to paint, and there were many details to include. Fortunately, my skills had improved considerably since the previous set of portraits and I was more adept at handling the more difficult passages of a painting. In these compositions, I strove to capture the sense of camaraderie at GAC and the importance of the work and social relationships that develop. While working in my studio, I would reflect upon what I knew about the lives of the people as I painted them. I thought a lot about what

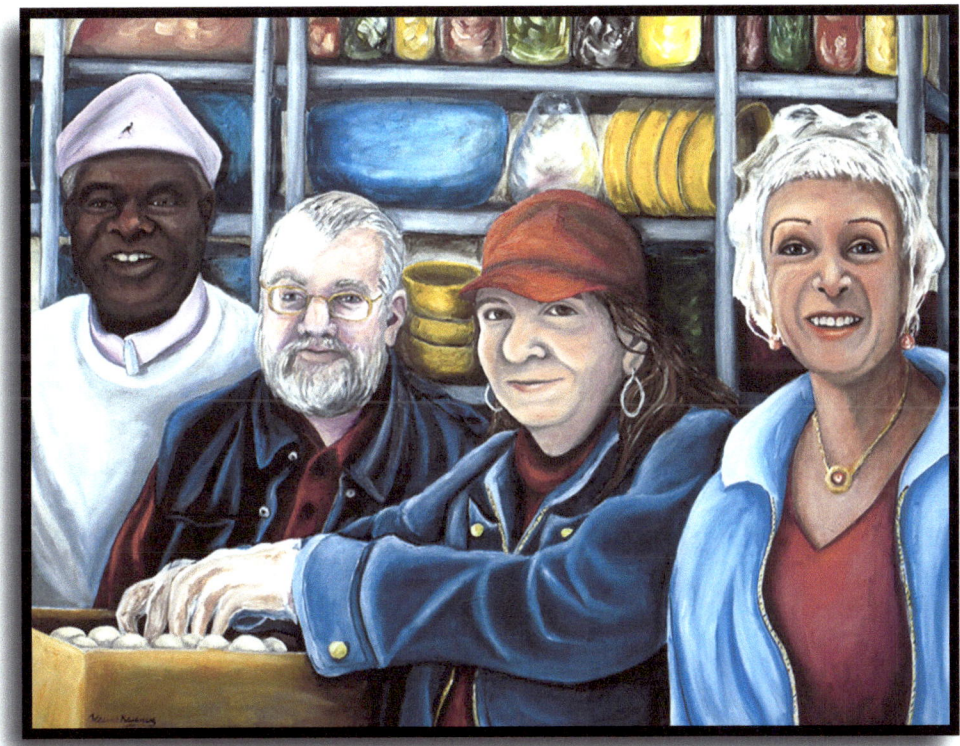

Preparing Lunch
Pictured from left to right:
James Wilborn, Michael Anderson, Cathy Duncan, Debbie Olson

recovery is about, how the movies and news media portray images of people who deal with mental illness in a negative manner, how art had the power to alter that image, and how creating a painting aligns with the process of recovery and reintegration after mental illness.

I created these portraits from photographic references and through personal observation of the members/subjects in their day to day lives at GAC. My technique involved using many layers of color applied

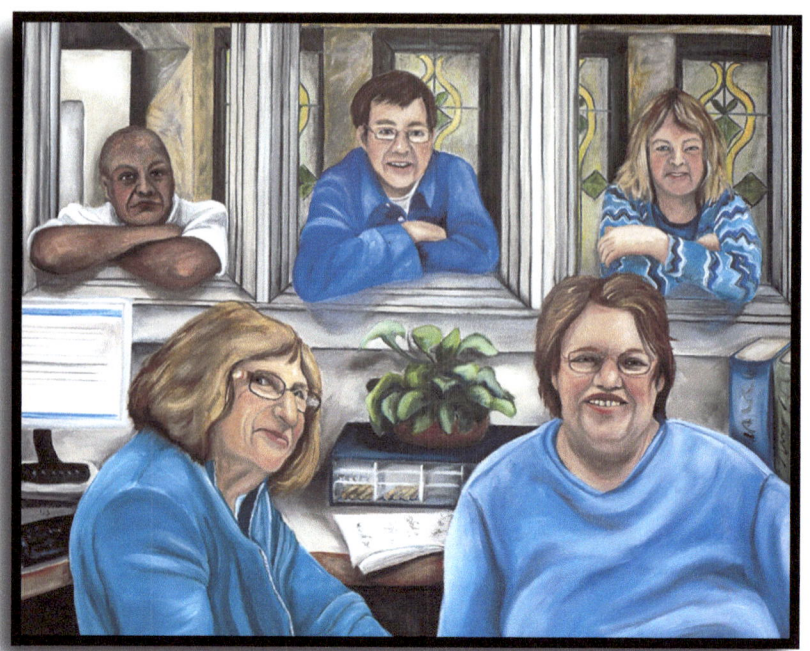

In the Office
Pictured top row, left to right:
Garfield Slaton, Joe Schanen, Linda Buddle
Pictured bottom row:
Diane Ullrich, April Rehor

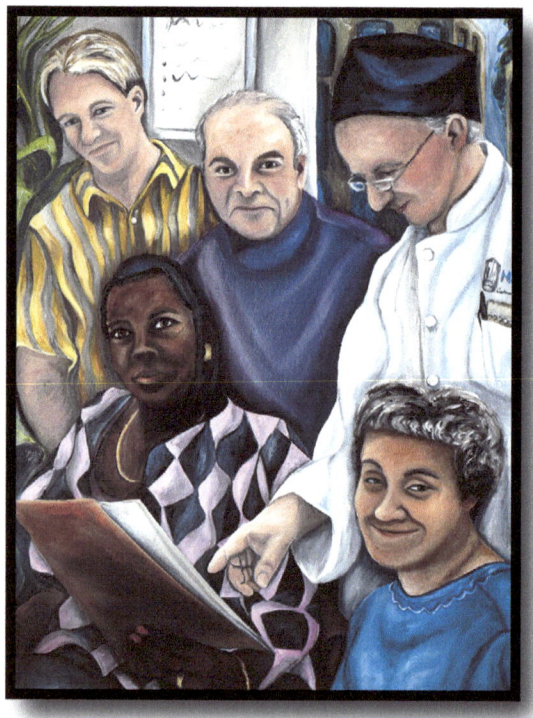

Planning Events
Pictured top row left to right:
Brian Graff, Amer Ariss, Glen Satterlund
Pictured bottom row:
Petra Thornton, Yolanda Velazquez

in varying stages of opaqueness. I started with a charcoal outline; the shadows were added and then the figure was "fleshed out" with skin tones. During this process the image started to form and the subjects residing in the painting began to emerge and take shape.

At this nexus of creation and observation, I perceived an important parallel between recovery and the process of creating my compositions. The melding of the varying elements in a portrait is much like the blossoming of a personality during recovery. There are bumps and starts, successes and mistakes, but in the end, the picture is completed. Like a portrait in the final stages of applying details and finishing touches, the person evolves and grows and emerges. After the elements have all been put in place the portrait—the person—is complete.

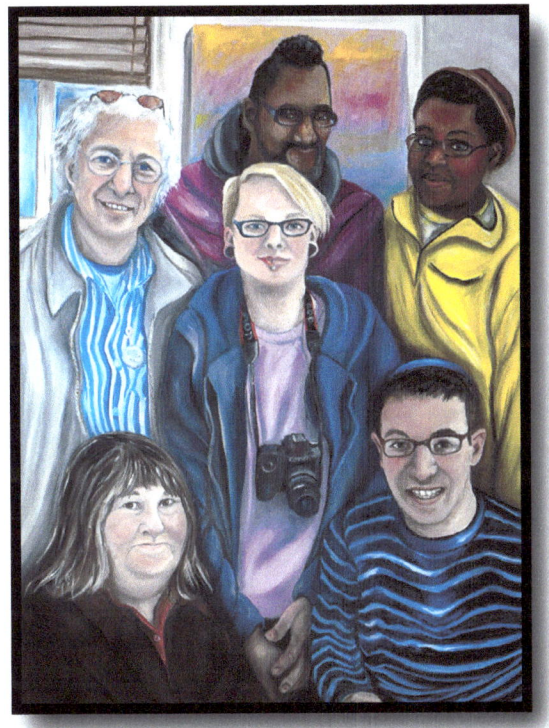

In the group portraits, some of the people portrayed I knew well and some, aware of the excitement associated with the project, showed up and announced that they were to be to be included in the picture! In all, I painted 51 people in the portraits, 20 in the individual portraits and 31 in the groups. The first phase of the project tells the narrative of the individual; the second phase reveals the people of a community and their relationships. The project in both phases humbled me, made me mature as an artist, and allowed me to leave behind, long after I am dust, the stories of the people who have touched my life so deeply.

In the Gallery

Pictured top row left to right:
Serge Blasberg, Earl Cooper, Grenesha Reed

Pictured middle: Tara Gulden
Pictured bottom row: Linda Shepard,
Michael Ish Shalom

In October of 2013, over two years of work and a lot of my soul went on display to a world-wide audience. All the portraits in both projects were exhibited at the *17th International Clubhouse Seminar* in St. Louis, Missouri. While there, Rachel Forman and I offered a seminar celebrating art as a vital addition to Clubhouse life.

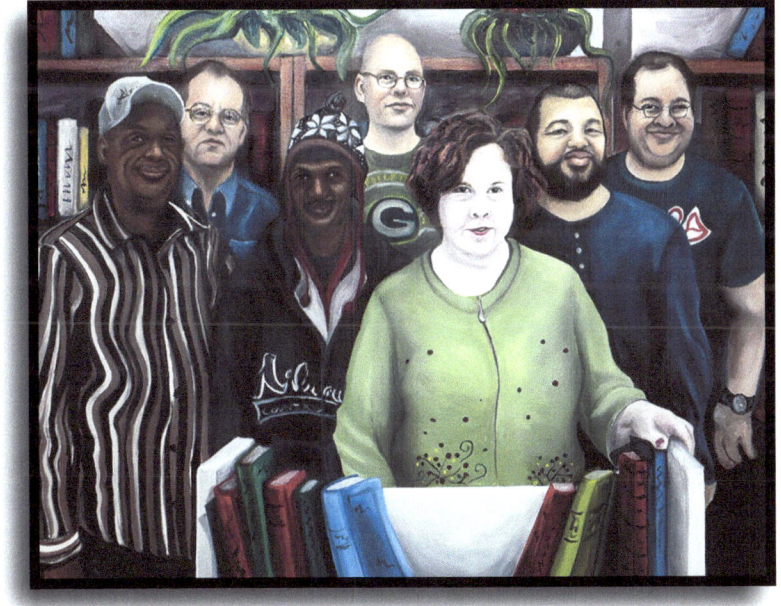

In the Library

Pictured top row left to right: John Manzuk, Chris Doering, Andrew Seny, Eric Risch
Pictured bottom row: Leroy Doyle, Walter Heard Jr., Jenny Hackbarth

The Blue Women

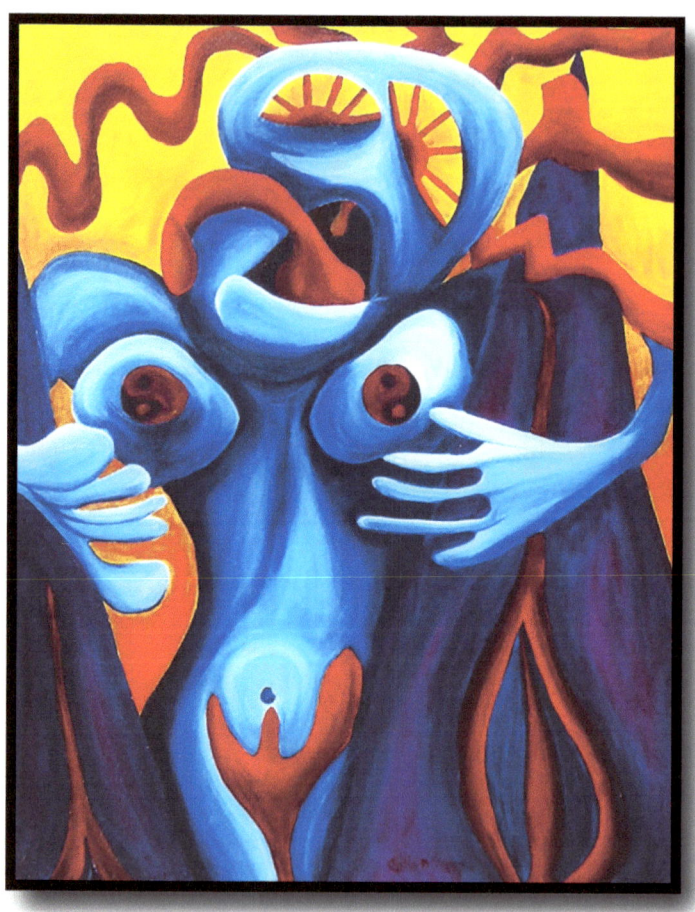

Psychiatry, ca. 2003

The *Blue Women* series was created after I returned home from a traumatic psychiatric hospitalization. I had been ill with uncontrolled diabetes for months and the symptoms were being misdiagnosed. When I entered the hospital my blood sugars were dangerously high and out of control. My complaints of illness were trivialized and ignored. More psych medications were prescribed to calm my "delusions" and "somatoform disorder." It took an astute nurse to see the glucose levels in my chart and to bring it to the attention of the psychiatrist. I was put on diabetes medications and sent home. The trauma of being seriously ill and not being heard because I was a psychiatric patient had left me exasperated and seething with anger. My trust in the medical/psychiatric system had been betrayed. This treatment wasn't right and I felt the hospital should know about it. The doctors involved needed to be made aware of the symptoms of diabetes and to check for the illness when patients experience these symptoms. It was a vulnerable time after the hospitalization and it took an immense amount of courage and strength on my part to go to the head of the department with my complaint. It was after this experience that I made a vow to never have another psychiatric hospitalization—one I have kept.

Psychiatry, is the first painting of this series. It was born late one night, when I woke crying in frustration because my complaint to the hospital was taking a long time to resolve. Philo told me to go into the studio and "paint it out." A blank canvas was already on the easel so I grabbed a brush full of red paint and painted the stripes on the canvas, yellow was applied to the background, and then purple was applied for the mountains. An intense blue was selected for the figure that is seen ripping aside the mountains to climb through and surmount them. I see this painting as an allegory of my hospital experience.

Blue Women has become the genre that speaks to my interpretations of feminine power and strength. The pieces have matured through time. Included in this book are six paintings representing the evolution of the series.

The painting, *Fecund,* is the last painting of this series that is done in acrylic. The seated figure is nestled in a lotus and embraces a seed pod ripe with fertility. It was painted after experiencing several years of stability and expressed my artistic emergence. Soon after completing this work I switched to oil paints. The first *Blue Woman* done in this medium is *Contemplation*. She is an abstracted figure resting in a garden of calla lilies, calm and reposed in thought. She was completed shortly after my return to GAC when I was wondering about where my work would be heading with this renewed involvement. The next two paintings in the series, *Wisdom* and *Balance* express the continuation of my emotional experiences working with GAC. I had reached a point of *Wisdom*—self-confidence so-to-speak—in my work and now felt that I wanted to give to others because of my recovery. It is *Balance* that conveys the delicate symbiosis of my sense responsibility to members of GAC and my art. It is a balance as precarious as the bubbles that rest upon her fingertips.

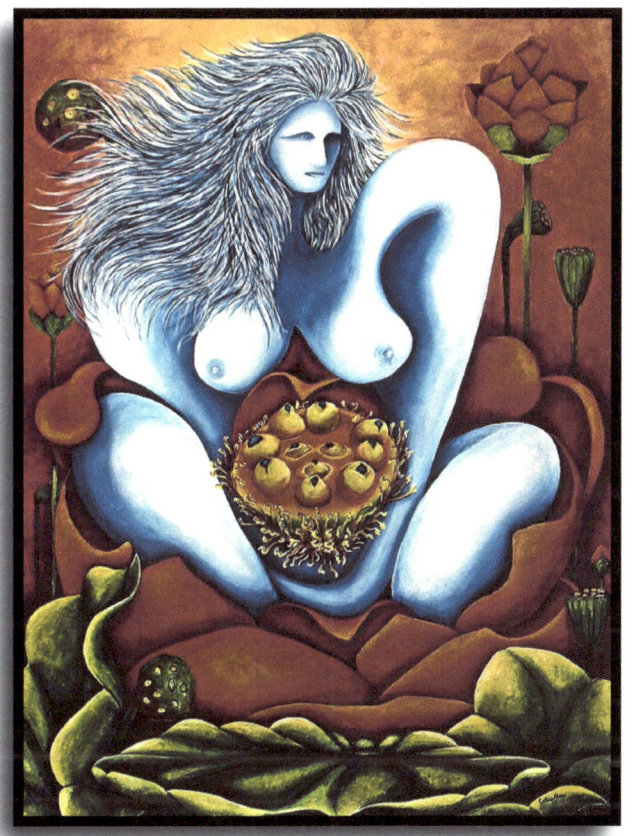

Fecund ca. 2003-04

With my most recent addition to the series, *Strength*, I envisioned a woman arising from an inferno and coming into the light. In the painting she has chains binding her to the burning earth beneath, yet, in her grasp they become flowered vines. She triumphs. She has climbed from the depths of hell into the light. It portrays what I know to be true. That a woman has great power, she can overcome many obstacles, she is beautiful in her own right, and can carry this light and beauty to others.

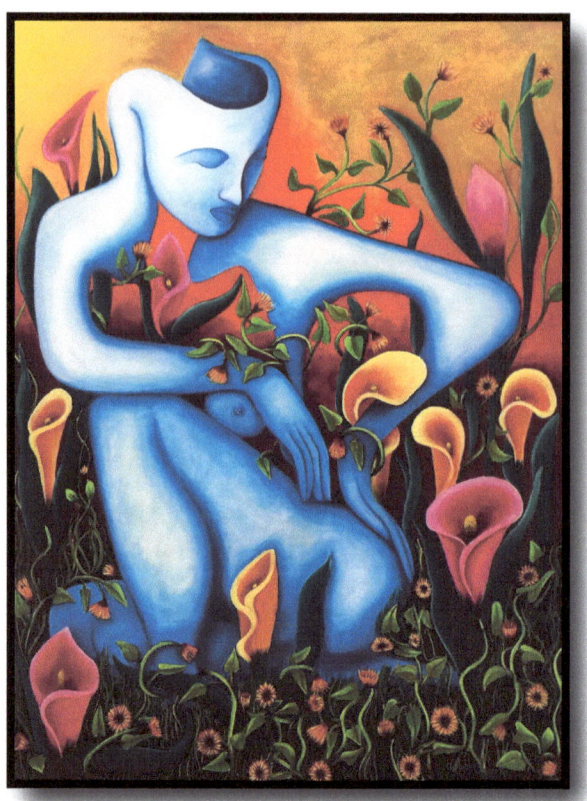

Contemplation, 2007—2008

The images in the *Blue Woman* series were born from a very painful time. Their evolution in both style and medium reflect my journey from beginning artist, to one discovering her way, to the artist I am today. The journey has been a long one. Where it will head from here? That is unknown. I do know this; the series will continue to grow and evolve just as I will as a human being. This is the most amazing part of life. It's always growing and always changing.

Diana Massey, one of my students at GAC modeled for the painting, *Strength*. I did not know her story when she posed and I had no idea how appropriate the title of this painting was to Diana's story. I am glad I am able to work with her and other GAC members, helping them to grow and develop the same love of art that I enjoy.

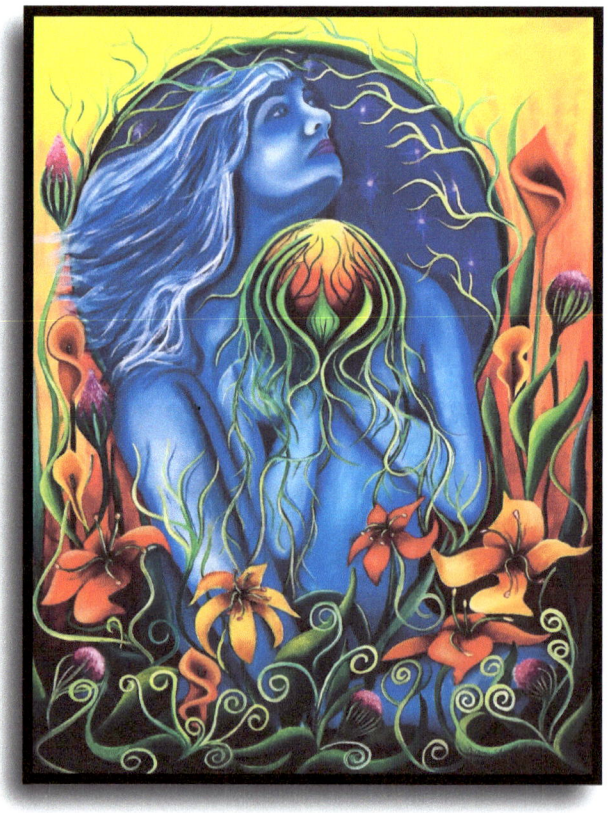

Wisdom, 2011

"I found out about my mental illness when I was diagnosed with breast cancer in 2010. For the ten years before that, I was a recovering addict. With the help of a loving husband and family, I have successfully stayed sober and have conquered a learning disability. Overcoming these issues has given me a strength that helps me to deal with the challenges life presented to me. I feel now that all the achievements I'm making were always within me.

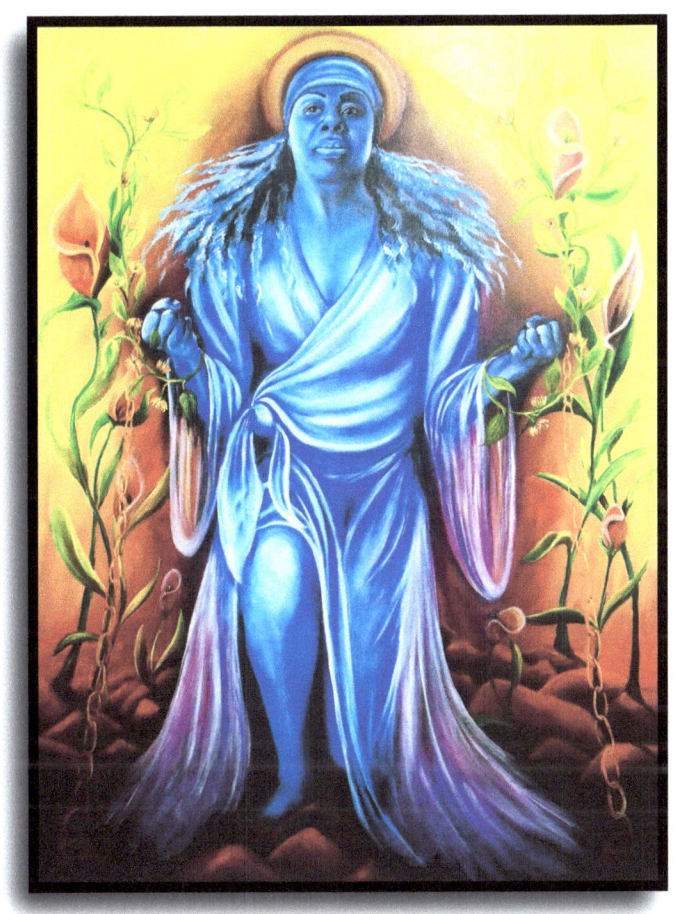

Strength, 2015

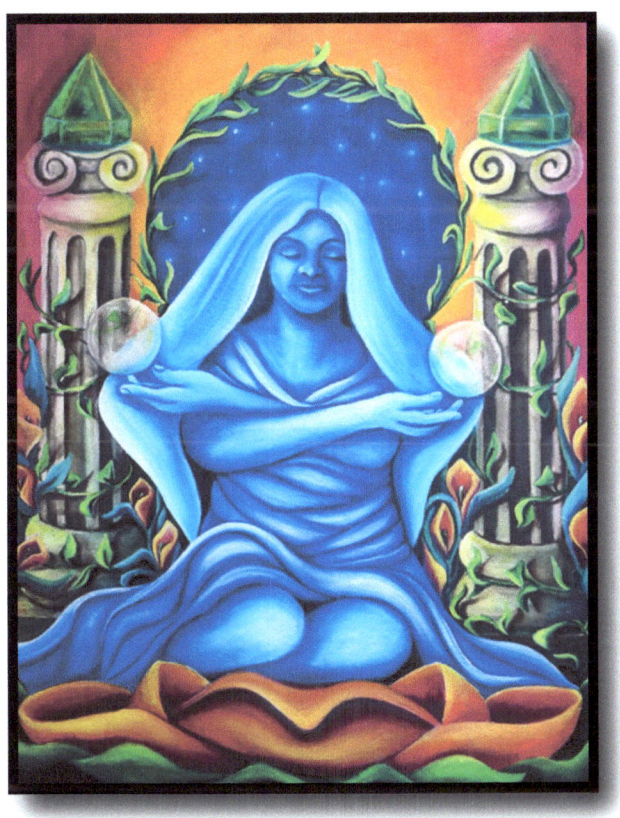

Balance, 2012

"I was always doing sketches or drawing and it made me feel whole. I never knew that I would actually be in gallery shows and that people would love and admire my talent. I never imagined having the strength that art has given me to heal. Art really works!"—Diana Massey

Wizened Women:

New Works

Womanhood—the lives of women, the emotions of women, and the strength of women—is a continuing theme in my painting. We are a remarkable gender. We are mothers, daughters, sisters, wives, lovers, and partners, keepers of the home and leaders of nations. We can laugh at ourselves, cry for another, and we endure.

My coming of age years were in the mid-1960—70's. *Women's Lib* was a new movement. The women leading the way were iconic. Gloria Steinem wrote eloquently, "like a man." Betty Friedan challenged our "mystique." Angela Davis strove to make black beautiful and powerful. Janis Joplin wailed the blues, Carol Burnett made us laugh, and Archie Bunker had to deal with Gloria. They were turbulent times and they were a changin'.

Many years have passed since then. The icons of my time are dead, aging, or have been forgotten. I'm older, wiser, and nervous about the future.

Today we are a global community. Technology has made communication instantaneous. I can hold a world of information in the palm of my hand. This globalism makes one acutely aware of the plight of people throughout the world. More than 50% of those people are women, a good portion of whom cannot or are not allowed to enjoy the freedoms I take for granted. I am now conscious of a world in which women are shrouded, mutilated, discriminated against, and still considered the property of a man. Often, it leaves me feeling helpless.

We need now, in this day and this world, to bond together as a gender—as humans—to become a world-wide network of support, leadership, and hope for our next generations. I am hopeful that this new generation soon will discover leaders as strong, as vocal, and as persistent as the women who influenced and led my youth.

The art I create may seem small when compared to the scope of the world's problems. It is, however, not insignificant. It is an interpretation of my world that is shared with others. If it can speak to the "humane-ness" of people, if it can tell stories of courage and hope, if it touches some chord within the viewer's psyche, I am happy. I have done my job.

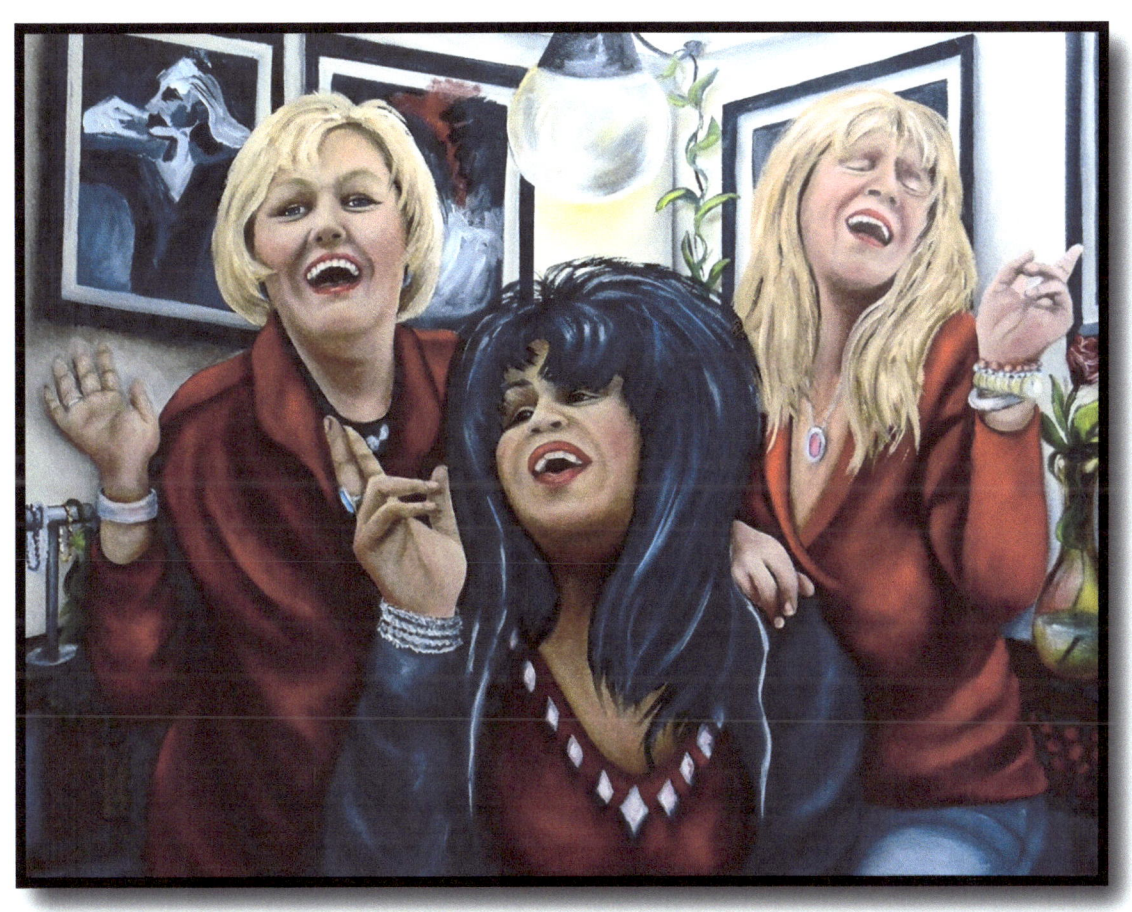

Girls Just Having Fun, 2014
Colleen Kassner, Stonie Rivera, Carol Rode-Curley

Della Wells

"During the 1950's and the 1960's most of the schools I attended were in Milwaukee. It was not because Milwaukee was great on race relations but because the African American community was a small prior to the 1950s. During the 1960's the African American population began to increase and segregation in the Milwaukee Pubic Schools began. Though my mother was from the South and my father was from Maryland, like so many African American parents of that era, they never talked about racism and segregation. My father only had two discussions with me about racism. I was seventeen and I wanted to go to Mississippi with my friends. My father told me no. I asked why. He responded, "You might get lynched!" The other time was when I was dating a young man who wore a jacket that had on the back of it, "I am black and proud!" My father told me, "...Do not bring that militant to his house again!" The young man later became a minister.

"I witnessed on television the horrors that Dr. King and the others in the Civil Rights Movement faced so African Americans could gain rights. I did not understand why we, as black people, were hated so much. I did not understand how children could be murdered: like Emmett Till, the four young girls who were killed in the church bombing, why dogs were put on the marchers and why they were beaten. Moreover, I did not understand the pain my parents must have felt regarding being Black in America. I am grateful for Dr. King and others who fought for civil rights for African Americans. We, today, owe them a lot. While things are not perfect, we must remember it will take each generation to move the goal post closer to freedom and equality for all men and women."
—Della Wells

I met Della several years ago when I called her to participate in a show Gallery Grand was producing for International Women's Day. Reluctant at first, she agreed to participate when she found that many of the artists in the show were people we both knew. Since that day, we've become friends. Della shows with Gallery Grand regularly and in 2010 guest curated a show for us, "Artists who Tell Stories." The show coincided with a First Stage Milwaukee production of *Don't Tell me I Can't Fly*, a children's play written by Y York and inspired by Della's life story.

Della is the first portrait in the *Wizened Women* series. The series originally was going to be called, *Water Women*, but it evolved as it went along. When I called Della about being in a portrait for this series, I asked whether it would be acceptable to show her holding water. She said, "Of course! I'm a Pisces!"

I photographed Della in my backyard on a sunny July afternoon. The photo was used for reference and many elements of her portrait are derived from my imagination.

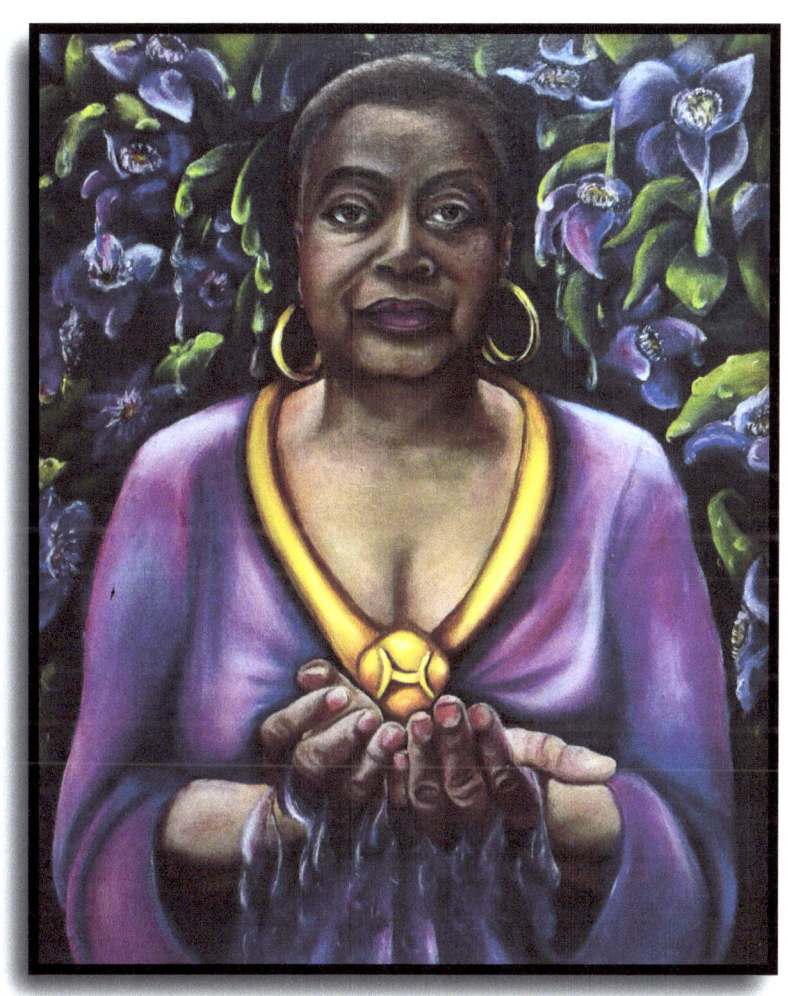

Della Wells, 2014

Debra Fabian

"I am a tribal member of the Oneida Nation of Wisconsin and I'm also of German, French and English bloodlines. I feel the strongest connection to my Native ancestors. I have had a love of rocks, trees, birds, flower gardens, animals, strawberries and maple syrup since I was a child. Honor all that has been given to us. Honor our fire, the spirit within each of us."—Debra Fabian

Deb has become a good friend over the past few years. She is a sculptor and upholsterer. She shows her whimsical furniture creations at Gallery Grand. We all fondly remember her chair "Grandma's Lap," which she exhibited for our first *International Women's Day* show.

Deb is one of the artists in an eclectic group of artists who meet on Friday nights. Together we discuss life, art, other artists, the art scene, Hollywood gossip, music, politics, and our lives. As a cozy circle of kindred spirits, we can laugh, share our woes and successes, and be with friends. We call it our "Prayer Meeting."

She is the second woman in the series. The late July summer was lush and verdant at this point. I captured her photo in during the mid–afternoon sun, again in our backyard. In her hands she is holding a shell she uses in her Native ceremonies. In the background hangs an eagle feather.

I did not know this, but it is illegal to have one unless you are Native.

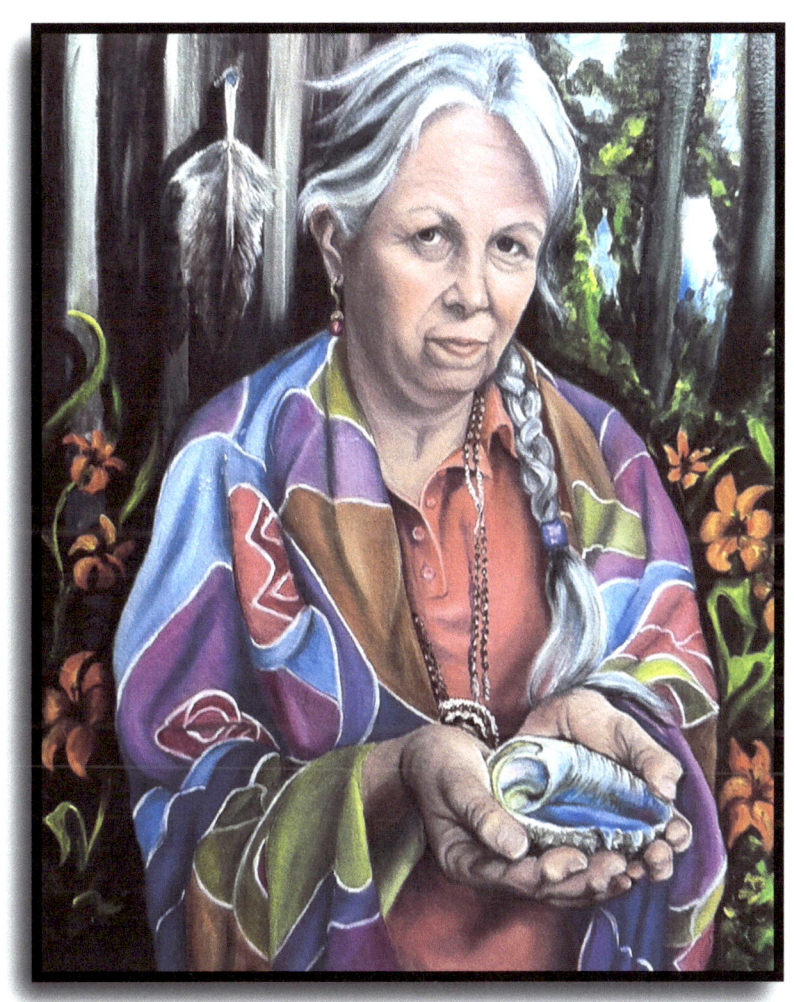

Debra Fabian, 2014

Susie Krause

"I have a quiet strength that I feel Colleen has captured in my portrait.

"I've had a weakened heart since early childhood, and spontaneously adjusted my activities to accommodate the condition. This does not mean I don't play or work hard. It just means I can't keep up the pace (in some instances) as long as I would like. In 2011 I had heart surgery to replace my aortic valve that was losing function. The valve replacement went well, but during surgery damage was done to my heart. A fierce battle was fought by my medical team, my partner, precious family, and dear friends to save my life. I also pushed hard to rehabilitate myself, and continue to do so.

"After the surgery, I experienced double vision. This was especially troubling to me because I am a painter. Over time my eyes have improved, and I regularly paint and draw. The beautiful hand-made brushes I hold in the painting were made by my partner Harvey. Together we inspire and motivate one another in our creative endeavors. Art, music, writing, family, photography, gardening, foraging and a deep appreciation of the real world inspire and sustain us."
—Susie Krause

It's hard to say "Susie" without saying "Susie and Harvey." They are an inseparable and delightful couple. They share many of the same interests that Philo and I do and have been our good friends for a long time. We do have our differences. They love forests, foraging, and nature; Philo and I love skyscrapers, neon, and concrete.

I photographed Susie in early August. The summer was already waning. She was surrounded by the trees in our backyard. When I took the photo, a beam of sunlight broke through the trees and illuminated her face, leaving the rest of her in lovely blue-green shadows. It is the lighting of a portraitist's dream.

She is holding paint brushes hand-made by Harvey. It is a lovely touch that seems to connect her to him through the painting.

Susie is a survivor. We almost lost her several years ago to a major heart problem. Her heart was repaired and her soul is as beautiful as ever.

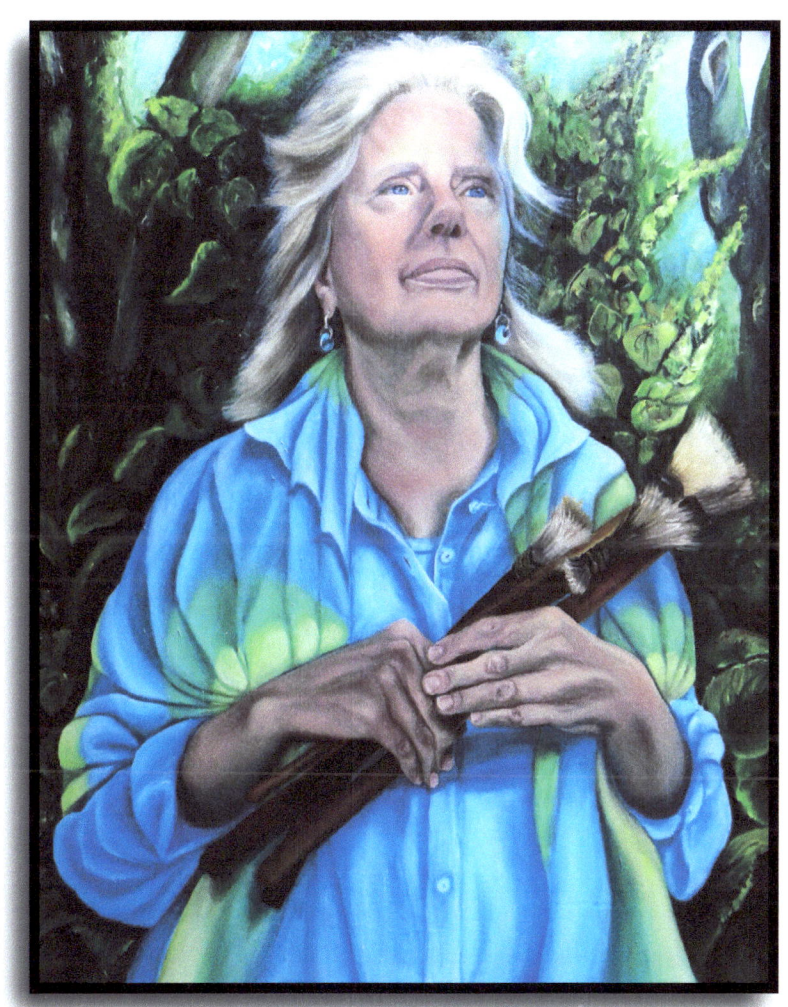

Susie Krause, 2014

Carol Rode–Curley

"My passion for drawing came from my father. He was an amazing cartoonist, sign painter, artist and comedian. It never occurred to me to do anything else. It's hard for me to put into words what I've been through, what I am going through and what I will go through, perhaps that's why I express my emotions through images... I don't know if I'm sane or not. I can't compare myself to anyone else, how can I, how can anyone?"—Carol Rode-Curley

I own one of Carol's pastels. It is how we met. She was showing at Dominion Gallery and I fell in love with the piece: *Red Lipped Ennui*. We became quick friends afterward.

When I asked her to model for the series, I stated that it was to be called the "Wizened Women." But, for her portrait only, I would rename it the *Wizened Women and the Wise-assed Woman*." It was said in loving jest and Carol thought it was an apt title. However, I sense Carol is far more complex and has many layers to her persona. She is a fabulous pastel artist, doing edgy portraits of women, often reflecting her inner realm; a place deep and unknown to many but alluded to through her artwork. She is also the fiercely proud mother of two teenagers who beautifully reflect her personality.

The photo for this portrait was taken in late August in glorious afternoon light. The clothing she wears is from my imagination and inspired by an illustrated book of women's clothing from the early 1900's. It is 100% Carol.

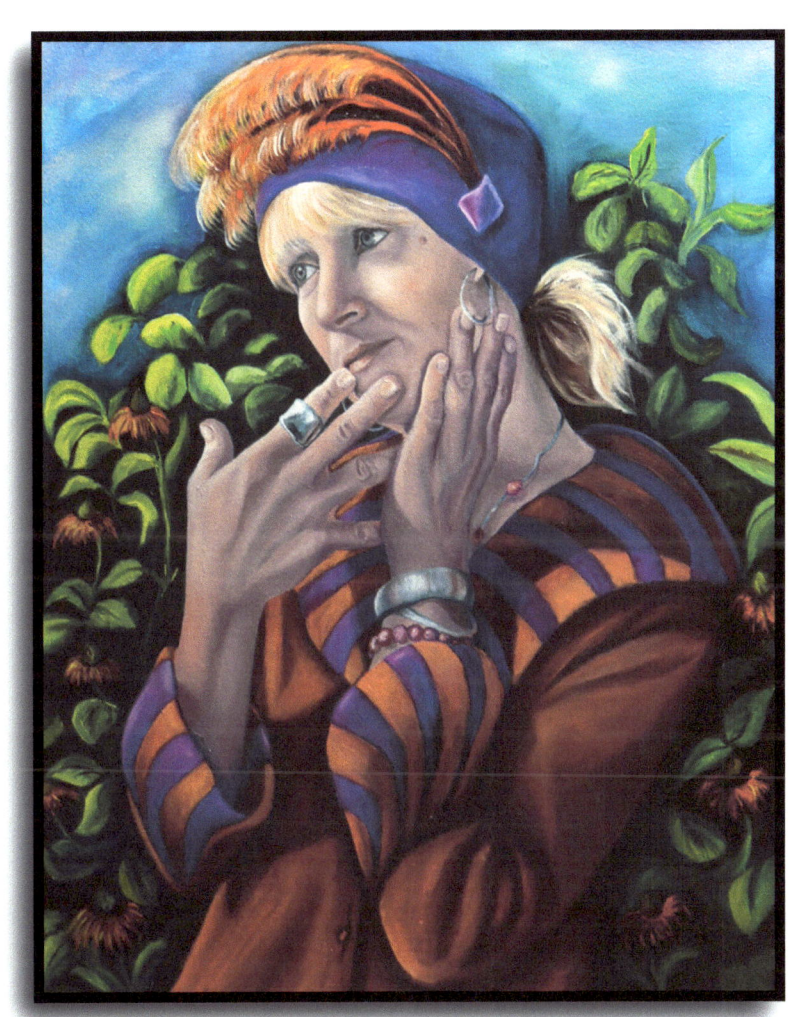

Carol Rode-Curley, 2014

Briana Shoop

"I like to surround myself with creative, outgoing, open minded people. I am a sucker for a political conversation, but don't like the fighting that it can sometimes bring, so I tend to, or try to, keep my mouth shut. When you do get me started, I am loud, opinionated, and UN-apologetic about my values, beliefs, and over all stances on society."—Briana Shoop

"I think the girl who is able to earn her own living and pay her own way should be as happy as anybody on earth. The sense of independence and security is very sweet." —Susan B. Anthony

Briana, my daughter, has grown into a lovely young woman and is a talented photographer. Her quotes on the opposite page are a perfect summary of the child I raised: a woman who is independent, self-assured, kind, just, hardworking, beautiful and creative.

Painting her portrait was a different experience from the others. At times it was bittersweet. I couldn't help but think of the years when I was so ill and how, as a teenager, she had to survive living with a parent with severe mental illness. It was very hard for her. They were difficult years, but they are in the past. I am a different person now. I hope that time and love have healed the wounds.

It is with pride and undying love that I created this painting. Capturing the light in Briana's eyes, the glow in her skin tones, and her lovely smile are my gift to her. I hope this love is evident in the painting and that it remains in her heart and life long after I am gone.

I took the photo for this painting in October, in our neighborhood, at the Riverside—Urban Ecology Center. The autumn colors were luminous in the late afternoon sun. Autumn is a beautiful season and Briana's favorite, the glow of autumn colors evident in her striking auburn hair.

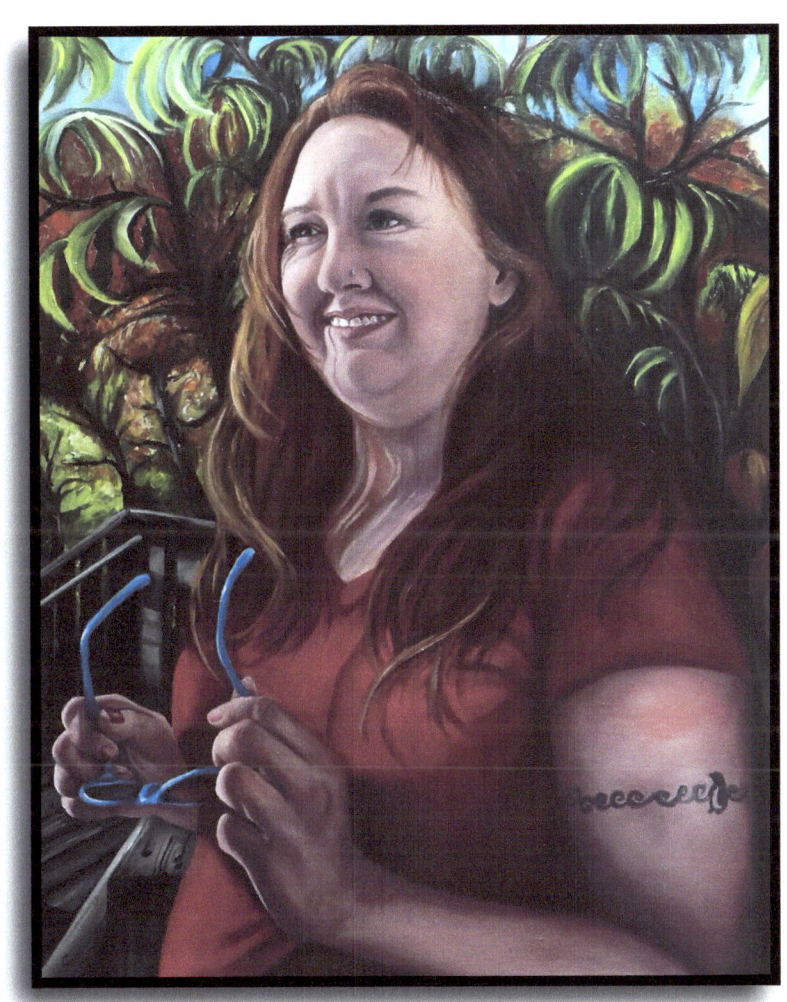

Briana Shoop, 2014

Stonie Rivera

"Not fitting in has always given me freedom, creativity, true self-expression and many great, odd, wonderful adventures."—Stonie Rivera

There are many words to describe Stonie Rivera: a woman of substance, mother, grandmother, punk rock musician, song writer, nurse, activist, artist, gallerist, world traveler, wife, psychic, author, and most of all, friend.

I met Stonie when purchasing my Carol Rode-Curley artwork at Dominion Gallery. Stonie ran Dominion with aplomb and a verve that was a joy to experience. We became instant friends. We found out a lot of our philosophies were the same. We were both active in advocating for mental health, she as a former psychiatric nurse, me as a social worker. She did a successful benefit for GAC in her gallery, which alas and sadly, is no more.

That doesn't stop Stonie! She now shows her photography at Gallery Grand and has become a good friend to us and a strong advocate of what we do at GAC. We are delighted to have her part of our family.

It was mid–September when I took this photo as the sun was thinning in the western sky. Stonie set up her crystal ball, her Tarot cards and candle, and the portrait was born.

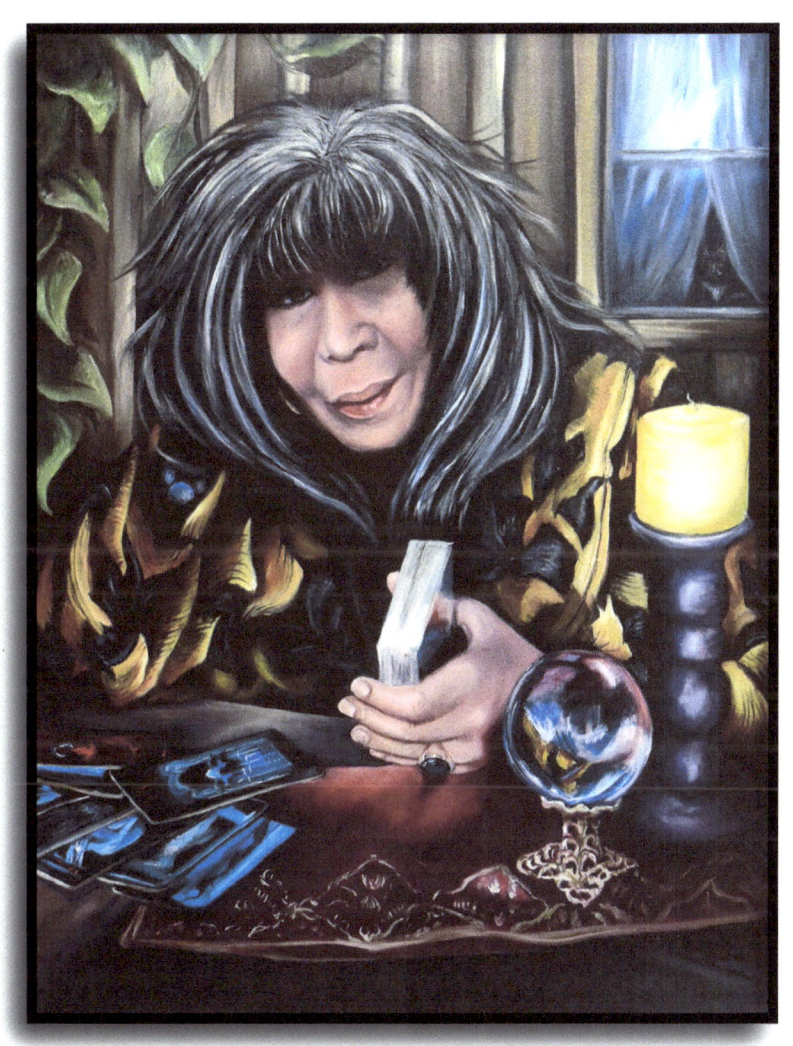

Stonie Rivera, 2015

I WANT TO BE PAINT

I place my passion
between oil and brush,
searching for meaning—
personhood—in visceral visions:
a face, the eyes, a Mona'ed grin.
Who is this before me
emerging from my vapored imaginings?

I can be paint.

Place me thick and glossy,
infused with aromatic linseed oil
upon this stark, barren canvas.

Give me the primary,
the primal backdrop used for
brush-strokes lifted from the palette:
vermilion, flaxen, cobalt.
Resounding passages of
impasto, layers of luminous glaze, and
nuanced light transmute into image:
a crimson detail,
a chalk-white speck,
a silent, violet shadow.

I paint.

I need no reason, no rhyme, nor verse.
I can be pigment,
be figment, be spectrum:
dreaming with eyes open,
no portrait of insanity.
This is life!

Revised, 2015

I wrote the original poem, *I Want to be Paint*, in 1995 and recently edited to reflect where I am today. It was created when the romance between Philo and me was starting to blossom. At the time, a gallery in Milwaukee was doing an art festival in its parking lot. It was filled with artists, poets, and a mélange of Milwaukeean Bohemia performing, displaying, and celebrating in the glorious July sun.

A long swath of paper and buckets of paint ran the length of the parking lot. It was set up for children but none were using it. That didn't last for long! Putting my bare feet in a glob of paint I proceeded to do a Cha-cha across the white paper leaving bright blue footprints in my wake. In a "Pied Piper" fashion, the children followed suit. Paint was everywhere and the peal of laughter could be heard all through the parking lot as we walked, slid, plopped and played in the paint.

Right after this it was my turn to read poetry. I sat at the edge of the stage; put my kaleidoscopic feet out in front of me, wiggled my multi-colored toes, and read.

It's when Philo knew I would become a painter.

The artwork selected for this book is/was part of the exhibit, *The Women behind the Paint: Colleen Kassner and Friends.* The theme of the artwork—the depiction of women and stories by or about them—was chosen to coincide with *International Women's Day* and *Women's History Month* in March of 2015 and exhibited in Gallery Grand @ GAC.

The introduction was written by Rachel Forman, who has become my dear friend, an inspiration to me, and a champion of my artwork. We met in the mid 1990's when I was a budding social work student. Our reconnection in 2006 was the beginning of a new life for me. Over the many wonderful years we have been associated, she has taught me much about courage, about exceeding my expectations, and setting my goals beyond the immediate. She is a woman of vision, loved by the GAC community, and the receiver of my utmost respect.

If you wish to learn more about Grand Avenue Club, Gallery Grand @ GAC, about the Clubhouse movement, or to contact me personally, you can go to these websites or emails below:

www.grandavenueclub.org

gallerygrand.org

www.clubhouse-intl.org

gallerygrand.gac@gmail.com